BIGGEST AND BEST OF CANADA

BIGGEST AND

BEST OF CANADA

1000 FACTS AND FIGURES

AARON KYLIE

FIREFLY BOOKS

A FIREFLY BOOK

Published by Firefly Books Ltd. 2014

First printing

Publisher Cataloging-in-Publication Data (U.S.)
Kylie, Aaron.
Canadian geographic biggest and best of Canada : 1000 facts & figures / Aaron Kylie.
[256] pages : col. ill. ; cm.
Includes index.
ISBN-13: 978-1-77085-279-2 (pbk.)
1. Canada--Miscellanea. I. Title. II. Biggest and best of Canada.
971.002 dc 23   FC61.K954 2014

Library and Archives Canada Cataloguing in Publication
Kylie, Aaron, author
Canadian geographic biggest and best of Canada : 1000 facts & figures / Aaron Kylie.
Includes index.
ISBN 978-1-77085-279-2 (pbk.)
1. Canada–Miscellanea–Pictorial works. I. Title.
II. Title: Biggest and best of Canada. III. Title: Canadian geographic.
FC61.K95 2014   971.002   C2014-901152-0

Published in the United States by
Firefly Books (U.S.) Inc.
P.O. Box 1338, Ellicott Station
Buffalo, New York 14205

Published in Canada by
Firefly Books Ltd.
50 Staples Avenue, Unit 1
Richmond Hill, Ontario L4B 0A7

Cover and interior design: Gareth Lind, LINDdesign.com

Printed in Canada

The publisher gratefully acknowledges the financial support for our publishing program by the Government of Canada through the Canada Book Fund as administered by the Department of Canadian Heritage.

Right: The Confederation Bridge linking Prince Edward Island and New Brunswick (see page 98).

Following page: The Dempster Highway that travels between Dawson, Yukon and Inuvik, Northwest Territories (see page 166).

INTRODUCTION

The best of Canada. For those who love the nation, there's so much to appreciate in this country. As the editor of *Canadian Geographic*, I have the privilege of exploring the best of Canada every day. The magazine, founded by the Royal Canadian Geographical Society, has been celebrating the nation for nearly 85 years, since its very first issue in May 1930. Its mandate is to make Canada better known to Canadians and the world.

Canadian Geographic shares the interesting people and places and the wildlife and wonders of the country, but the focus of this book is the exploration of what is best in Canada: the biggest, tallest, highest and longest, as well the firsts and the world bests. *The Biggest and Best of Canada* is a compendium of Canadian superlatives, from the nation's geography and weather to its animals and communities, its innovations and amazing people. It covers the gamut of the nation's most notable aspects, with sections on all of these topics, as well as business and industry, transportation, communication, pop culture, sports and leisure, other miscellaneous feats and renowned roadside attractions.

In terms of geography, few items are as noteworthy as the world's oldest rocks (page 18). In 2008, researchers from Canada and the United States discovered that rocks from along the coast of Hudson Bay in northern Quebec are about 4.28 billion years old. If you think old rocks aren't exciting, take heed of the statement made in the journal *Science* by Jonathan O'Neil, the lead author of the study: "Our discovery not only opens the door to further unlock the secrets of the Earth's beginnings. Geologists now have a new playground to explore how and when life began, what the atmosphere may have looked like, and when the first continent formed."

Signal Hill, Saint John's, Newfoundland (see page 126).

When it comes to weather, we all know Canada is snowy and cold (and we have the records to back it up!), but Canadians also invented, of all things, the UV Index (page 65). The Ultraviolet Index is, according to Environment Canada, "a measure of the intensity of the sun's ultraviolet radiation in the sunburn spectrum." It was created by Environment Canada researchers in 1992 to help Canadians appreciate the severity of sunburn when they are exposed to ultraviolet radiation. Subsequently, other countries around the world developed similar indexes.

The story of Canada's first zoo (page 79) is particularly interesting. Established in Halifax by naturalist Andrew Downs in 1847, the Down's Zoological Gardens was a favourite destination for visitors to the city. Famed sportsman Campbell Hardy said this about it: "Every visitor desirous of acquaintance with wild life in the woods or water of Acadie, went to Downs for advice or reference." What of the zoo today? It was sold in 1867 and ultimately became New York's Central Park Zoo.

You might be surprised by the location of a significant number of Canada's record-setting structures — Montreal. The city is home to the eighth-tallest building in the country (page 86), the largest hockey arena (page 89), the largest stadium (page 88), the largest church (page 89), the largest cemetery (page 89), the continent's first commercial movie theatre (page 90) and the nation's busiest bridge (page 98). No wonder UNESCO named it a City of Design in 2006.

If you're a fan of hotdogs, you'll be happy to learn that Saskatchewan is the world's largest producer of mustard (page 112). What Canadian wouldn't be proud of this proclamation from the Saskatchewan Mustard Development Commission: "The Canadian mustard industry is supported by the most experienced scientific development and research teams, and employs the most technologically advanced production methods in the world." Who knew?

Canada is home to one of the world's leading publishers of books for women (page 125). Toronto-based Harlequin Romance had 92 titles spend a combined total of 313 weeks on the *New York Times* best-seller lists in 2012. And four titles nabbed the Number-One spot. The company sells 95 percent of their books outside Canada and Harlequin has offices in 12 international cities, from Sydney, Australia, to London, England.

When it comes to innovations, the nation clearly has a refined palette — at least if you consider the number of edible advancements that have come from Canada. There's the McIntosh (page 134) and Spartan (page 134) apples, Red Fife (page 135) and Marquis (page 135) wheat, canola (page 135), the continent's first chocolate nut bar (page 135), frozen fish (page 134), Pablum (page 134), peanut butter (page 137), Canada Dry (page 137), Yukon Gold (page 136) and Shepody (page 136) potatoes and the Bloody Caesar (page 136). And Canadians are also responsible for dozens of non-edible inventions.

For some reason, the province with the most roads is Saskatchewan (page 164). It has the most road surface in Canada, with 250,000 km of roadways. Saskatchewan has the most roads per capita of any place in the world. The vast majority of the roads are gravel, with paved municipal roads making up less than 1 percent of the province's roadways (just 1,500 km). It seems that not only can you see for miles on the Prairies, but you can drive for hundreds of them, too.

There's little question as to why Canada has earned the moniker "Hollywood North." After all, the first kiss in movie history (page 176) involved a Canadian, the first Hollywood star to be known by her real name (page 177) was Canadian, one of the founders of Warner Bros. Pictures (page 177) was Canadian, and the first actress with a star on the Hollywood Walk of Fame (page 176) was Canadian. The first Oscar for a documentary film (page 178) was won by a Canadian, the only siblings to win Oscars in the same year (page 179) were Canadians and the writer and director of the two top-grossing movies ever (page 179) is a Canadian. The oldest actor to win an Oscar (page 178) is Canadian, and the famed Hollywood sign itself was built by a Canadian (page 176).

Canadians seem to have a talent for creating sports. The country is the birthplace of hockey (page 192), lacrosse (page 198), ringette (page 199) and 5-pin bowling (page 207). And a Canadian invented basketball (page 202). While the nation may not be able to lay claim to the origin of baseball, the first recorded baseball game (page 206) was played in Beachville, Ontario, legend Babe Ruth hit his first professional home run in Toronto (page 206), and Jackie Robinson, the first black baseball player in Major League Baseball's modern era, played his first professional games in Montreal (page 206). Oh, and Montreal's McGill University played in the first "American" football game in the world.

There are hundreds more of these biggest and best facts and figures about Canada in the pages that follow. As a collection of Canadian claims to fame, this book celebrates the nation in all its superlative grandeur.

Alberta's Dinosaur Provincial Park (see page 39).

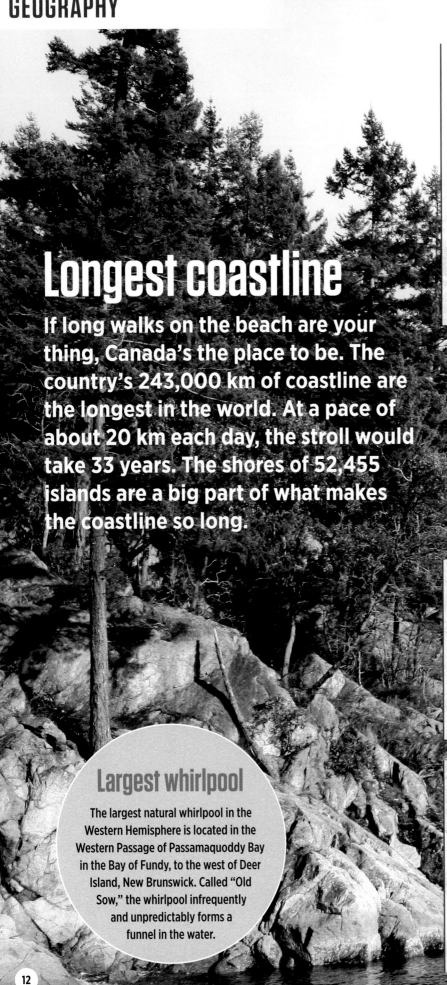

Longest coastline

If long walks on the beach are your thing, Canada's the place to be. The country's 243,000 km of coastline are the longest in the world. At a pace of about 20 km each day, the stroll would take 33 years. The shores of 52,455 islands are a big part of what makes the coastline so long.

Richest sea harvest

Considered one of the world's largest and richest resource areas, the Grand Banks off the southeast coast of Newfoundland have been plumbed for resources since at least the 1400s. The banks are actually a series of raised underwater plateaus ranging between 36.5 and 185 m deep. The relatively shallow water allows a range of marine and plant life to thrive. Fishermen from around the Atlantic harvest haddock, ocean perch, crabs, clams and scallops, as well as hundreds of other species from these waters.

Largest northern inland sea

Hudson Bay is considered the world's largest northern inland sea. It covers 822,324 square km. It's the world's second-largest bay, and the largest if measured by coastline, at 12,268 km.

Largest wetland

The Hudson Bay Lowland is the largest wetland area in North America and the third largest on Earth. Eighty-three percent of the ecozone lies in Ontario, with smaller portions in neighbouring Quebec and Manitoba. More than 85 percent of the region is mineral wetland or organic peat land. The area has very few trees.

Largest whirlpool

The largest natural whirlpool in the Western Hemisphere is located in the Western Passage of Passamaquoddy Bay in the Bay of Fundy, to the west of Deer Island, New Brunswick. Called "Old Sow," the whirlpool infrequently and unpredictably forms a funnel in the water.

Highest tides

Sure, Canada's Bay of Fundy has the highest tides in the world, but did you know that at some times of year the difference between low and high tide can be taller than a three-storey building? Indeed, Fundy's tides can differ by up to 16.27 m. Part of the reason for Fundy's dramatic tides are the V-shape of the bay, which funnels water into less and less space causing the water to rise.

Highest variation between tides

Speaking of tides, the world's highest variation between high and low tide — 16.27 m — was recorded at Burntcoat Head, Nova Scotia, in Minas Basin on the Bay of Fundy. The average tide there is 10 m.

Largest estuary

With water flowing out from the Great Lakes, the largest source of freshwater in the world, it's little wonder the St. Lawrence maritime estuary (a place where fresh and saltwater mix) is one of the largest and deepest estuaries in the world. Freshwater increasingly mixes with saltwater for nearly 250 km, from Île d'Orléans, near Quebec City, to Pointe-des-Monts, northeast of Baie Comeau on the St. Lawrence River's north shore.

Largest continuous wetland

The Columbia Wetlands, located on the Upper Columbia River in the East Kootenays area of British Columbia, are considered the largest continuous wetlands in North America. The wetlands cover some 15,000 hectares over a 150 km stretch, from Canal Flats and Invermere to Golden.

Largest erratic

A big rock, indeed. Known as "The Big Rock," the Okotoks Erratic (a rock moved from its original location by a glacier) is the largest known glacial erratic in the world. Weighing an estimated 16,500 tonnes, and measuring about 9 m high, 41 m long and 18 m wide, the Big Rock is located southwest of Okotoks, Alberta. It's believed the erratic was originally part of a mountain in what is now Jasper National Park, some 450 km away.

HIGHEST POINT
Alberta

At an elevation of 3,747 m, Mount Columbia in Banff National Park is the highest point in Alberta. (It's also the second-highest point in the Canadian Rockies).

Highest mountains

Look up, way up ... to Canada's highest mountains!

	Name	Height	Location
1.	Angel Peak, British Columbia	6,858 m	58.486 / –124.859
2.	Mount Logan, Yukon	5,959 m	60.567 / –140.403
3.	Mount Lucania, Yukon	5,226 m	61.022 / –140.463
4.	King Peak, Yukon	5,173 m	60.583 / –140.654
5.	Mount Steele, Yukon	5,073 m	61.093 / –140.3
6.	Mount Wood, Yukon	4,842 m	61.233 / –140.512
7.	Mount Vancouver, Yukon	4,812 m	60.359 / –139.698
8.	Mount Slaggard, Yukon	4,742 m	61.173 / –140.584
9.	Mount Hubbard, Yukon	4,557 m	60.319 / –139.071
10.	Mount Walsh, Yukon	4,507 m	61 / –140.017

HIGHEST POINT
British Columbia

The highest point in British Columbia is Mount Fairweather, which sits at an elevation of 4,663 m. It's located on the Alaska border at the southern end of the province's Tatshenshini-Alsek Wilderness Provincial Park. Captain James Cook named the mountain after he saw the peak in "fair weather" while exploring the region in 1778.

HIGHEST POINT
Northwest Territories

Seems a fitting name for this remote, spectacular mountain. Mount Nirvana is the highest point in the Northwest Territories, rising to to 2,773 m above sea level.

Longest cliff face

It really is a picture that speaks louder than words. It's difficult to describe the impressive sight of Mount Thor, a peak in Nunavut's Auyuittuq National Park. It has the world's longest uninterrupted cliff face, measuring approximately one km. The mountain, named after the Norse god of thunder, soars 1,675 m above sea level.

HIGHEST POINT
Prince Edward Island

It's likely little surprise that Canada's smallest province has its lowest highest point. This spot, located at Springton in Queen's County, Prince Edward Island, lies 142 m above sea level.

HIGHEST POINT Quebec

The highest point in Quebec is located along its border with Labrador in the province's northeast. Mont d'Iberville lies 1,652 m above sea level in Quebec's parc national Kuururjuaq.

HIGHEST POINT
Nova Scotia

Yet another appropriate name: Nova Scotia's highest point lies in the aptly named Cape Breton Highlands (pictured here). White Hill Lake in the Cape Breton Highlands National Park has an elevation of 532 m.

HIGHEST POINT
Saskatchewan

Since Saskatchewan is known for its expanse of flat prairie, it seems suitable that the highest point in the province is referred to as a hill. The Cypress Hills to be exact, located in the province's southwestern corner. The so-called "West Block" of the Hills, lying along the border with Alberta, has an elevation of 1,392 m. This geographical region extends into Alberta, where the highest point rises 1,466 m above sea level.

HIGHEST POINT
Newfoundland

About 20 km north of Stephenville, Newfoundland, on the island's west coast, you'll find the Rock's highest elevation, the Lewis Hills. Located along the coast at Port au Port Bay, the Hills sit 814 m above sea level.

HIGHEST POINT
New Brunswick

New Brunswick's Mount Carleton is not only the province's highest point, but also the highest point in the Maritimes. From the 817 m elevation located in Mount Carleton Provincial Park, it's estimated you can see some 10 million trees. The mountain is named after the province's first governor, General Thomas Carleton.

HIGHEST POINT
Ontario

Ontario may boast the biggest and best of many things in the country, but its highest point is not one of them. Located in the Timiskaming area of northern Ontario, the Ishpatina Ridge is the province's highest spot, at an elevation of 693 m.

HIGHEST POINT
Labrador

It would seem that a mountain by any other name would still be as high. The highest point in Labrador is the same as Quebec's, although on the Labrador side of the border Mont d'Iberville is known as Mount Caubvik, at an elevation of 1,652 m.

HIGHEST POINT
Manitoba

The flat prairie plains of central Canada cover much of Manitoba. Still, Baldy Mountain, at an elevation of 831 m, is the province's highest point, lying in Duck Mountain Provincial Park. Visitors can drive to the top of the mountain and take in the surrounding region from a 12 m high observation tower.

Oldest rocks

The oldest known rocks on Earth—250 million years older than any other known rocks—are found in Canada. Geologists discovered the 4.28-billion-year-old rock in 2001 in an area of exposed bedrock on the eastern shore of Hudson Bay, in northern Quebec.

Perfect peak

It's Canada's perfect peak. British Columbia's Mount Assiniboine (3,618 m) is considered the Matterhorn of North America, due to its nearly symmetrical, pyramid shape.

Largest cave

The country's largest known cave system, Castleguard Cave, is located in Alberta's Banff National Park. The cave extends for 23 km below the Columbia Icefields. It is the world's only cave where some passages are plugged by ice pushed in from the surface. The cave's entrance tends to flood unexpectedly, so the cave can only be safely explored in winter.

Largest crater

The largest known impact crater in Canada (and the second-largest on Earth) is found near Sudbury, Ontario. Known as the Sudbury Basin, the crater is 130 km in diameter. It is believed that the impact of a 10 km meteorite created the Sudbury Basin in just seconds about 1.85 million years ago.

Oldest part of North America

The Canadian Shield, which is about 4.4 million square km in size, covers about half of Canada and encircles Hudson Bay, was the first part of North America permanently above sea level. It is also the oldest section of the continent's crustal plate (a layer of the Earth's surface) and the largest area of exposed Precambrian rock (formed about 500 million years ago) on

Largest karst

This is one impressive drain. The Maligne Valley karst is the largest known underground drainage system in the country. Located in Alberta's Jasper National Park, the drainage includes Medicine Lake and Maligne Canyon.

Highest pingo

The Ibyuk Pingo, near Tuktoyaktuk, Northwest Territories, is the highest pingo (a unique ice-core formation) in Canada and the second largest in the world. It pokes up 49 m above the surrounding terrain.

The most pingos

Our pingos are bigger than yours. The Northwest Territories' Mackenzie Delta region is home to the world's greatest concentration of pingos (some 1,350) and the largest. A pingo is an ice-cored hill, usually conically shaped, that grows only in permafrost. They're formed when water freezing under the surface is forced up by pressure, and they range from a few metres to several tens of metres high.

Largest non-polar icefield

The Yukon's Seward Glacier and Alaska's Bagley Icefield together form the largest non-polar icefield in the world. The area is home to some of the world's longest and most spectacular glaciers. The icefields are a United Nations Educational, Scientific and Cultural Organization (UNESCO) world heritage site that combines Kluane National Park and Reserve in the Yukon and Tatshenshini-Alsek Provincial Park in British Columbia with Wragell-St. Elias National Park and Glacier Bay National Park in Alaska.

Largest hot springs

The hot springs in the village of Radium Hot Springs, British Columbia, are the largest in the country. The pool's water, maintained at a temperature of 39°C, is odourless and clear.

21

Highest hydraulic lift lock

Talk about moving up in the world! Lock 21 on the Trent-Severn Waterway in Peterborough, Ontario, is the highest hydraulic lift lock in the world. Opened on July 9, 1904, the lock lifts boats 19.8 m. It was also the first of only two lift locks ever built in North America.

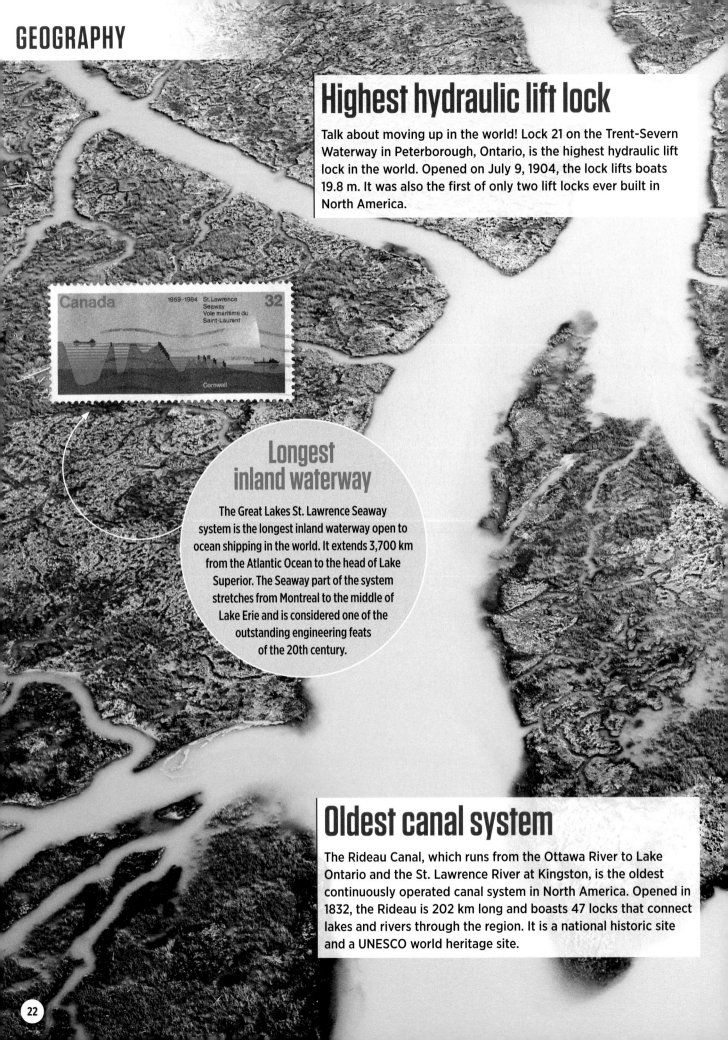

Longest inland waterway

The Great Lakes St. Lawrence Seaway system is the longest inland waterway open to ocean shipping in the world. It extends 3,700 km from the Atlantic Ocean to the head of Lake Superior. The Seaway part of the system stretches from Montreal to the middle of Lake Erie and is considered one of the outstanding engineering feats of the 20th century.

Oldest canal system

The Rideau Canal, which runs from the Ottawa River to Lake Ontario and the St. Lawrence River at Kingston, is the oldest continuously operated canal system in North America. Opened in 1832, the Rideau is 202 km long and boasts 47 locks that connect lakes and rivers through the region. It is a national historic site and a UNESCO world heritage site.

First lock canal

The canal at Coteau-du-Lac, Quebec, was the first lock canal in North America. Completed in 1781, three locks dropped the level of the canal approximately two metres. The canal provided a safe way to avoid the rapids, which measured about two metres from head to bottom.

Longest river system

It could be the nation's longest winding trail. The Mackenzie River system is Canada's longest waterway, from its origins in the Columbia Icefields in Alberta's Jasper National Park and the deep snowfields of the upper Peace River in northeastern British Columbia to its mouth on the Beaufort Sea of the Arctic Ocean on Nunavut's coast. Including all the rivers and lakes of the system's 1.8-million-square-km drainage basin, it stretches 4,241 km in total, ranking as the world's 13th-longest river system.

Canada's longest rivers

♦ 4,240 km	1. Mackenzie, Northwest Territories
♦ 3,060 km	2. St. Lawrence, Quebec/Ontario
♦ 2,580 km	3. Nelson, Manitoba
♦ 1,610 km	4. Churchill, Alberta/Saskatchewan/Manitoba
♦ 1,540 km	5. Peace, British Columbia/Alberta
♦ 1,370 km	6. Fraser, British Columbia (pictured here)
♦ 1,290 km	7. North Saskatchewan, Alberta/Saskatchewan/Manitoba
♦ 1,270 km	8. Ottawa, Quebec/Ontario
♦ 1,230 km	9. Athabasca, Alberta
♦ 1,150 km	10. Yukon (Canadian portion only), British Columbia/Yukon

Largest freshwater ecosystem

Looking for fresh water? Look no farther than the Great Lakes. Lake Ontario, Lake Erie, Lake Huron, Lake Michigan and Lake Superior form the world's largest freshwater ecosystem. It's estimated that a drop of water takes 400 years to travel from the system's headwaters in Lake Superior to the point where Lake Ontario meets the St. Lawrence River. The Great Lakes basin contains about 18 percent of the world's fresh lake water.

Largest high-elevation lake

The nation's largest, natural, high-elevation freshwater lake is British Columbia's Chilko Lake. The 158-square-km body of water sits at an elevation of 1,171 m.

More lakes

There are millions of lakes in Canada, so it's hardly surprising that our nation has more lake area than any other country. They're often big, too, with 563 lakes larger than 100 square km.

Oldest water

With all the water in Canada, is it any wonder that the oldest known water on the planet was found here? University of Toronto geoscientist Barbara Sherwood Lollar and her colleagues discovered the 2.6-billion-year-old water some 2.4 km below the earth in a mine near Timmins, Ontario.

Largest lake that drains two ways

Northeastern Saskatchewan's Wollaston Lake (2,681 square km) is the largest lake in the world that naturally drains in two directions. The Fond Du Lac River drains from Wollaston to the northwest into Lake Athabasca and the Mackenize River system, while the Cochrane River drains from the lake to the northeast into Reindeer Lake and the Hudson Bay basin.

One-third of Earth's fresh water

Given that the Great Lakes host the world's largest supply of fresh water, it's little surprise that the province where the lakes are found, Ontario (which is also home to more than 250,000 other lakes), contains about one-third of the Earth's fresh water.

Longest freshwater coast

Lake Huron, including Georgian Bay, has the longest freshwater coast of any lake in the world. It boasts 6,157 km of shoreline.

Largest freshwater lake

The greatest of the Great Lakes, Lake Superior is the largest freshwater lake in the world. It covers 82,100 square km, 28,700 of which are in Canada. It is 563 km long, 257 km wide and 406 m deep at its deepest point.

DEEPEST LAKE

At 614 m deep, Great Slave Lake in the Northwest Territories is North America's deepest lake. The 27,000 square km lake is also the second-largest lake in Canada and the ninth largest in the world.

Biggest continuous body of fresh water

The Great Lakes are the world's biggest continuous body of fresh water.

Biggest lake inside Canada

The Northwest Territories' Great Bear Lake is the biggest lake wholly in Canada, and the eighth-largest lake in the world. It has an area of 31,792 square km and is 1,470 m deep at its deepest spot.

Most Canadian Great Lake

Canada shares four of the Great Lakes with the United States (Lake Michigan is wholly in the United States). But do you know which lake has the largest portion in Canada? Lake Huron, with a total of 36,000 of its 59,600 square km north of the border.

Canada's 10 biggest lakes

1. Lake Huron, Ont.
2. Great Bear Lake, N.W.T.
3. Lake Superior, Ont.
4. Great Slave Lake, N.W.T.
5. Lake Winnipeg, Man.
6. Lake Erie, Ont.
7. Lake Ontario, Ont.
8. Lake Athabasca, Sask.
9. Reindeer Lake, Sask./Man.
10. Smallwood Reservoir, Nfld.

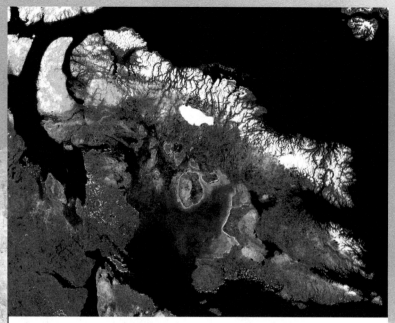

Largest inland freshwater delta

While such things are debatable because of the range of criteria on which they're based, nonetheless the Global Institute for Water Security considers the Saskatchewan River Delta—a series of lakes, rivers and wetlands along the Saskatchewan-Manitoba border—to be the largest inland freshwater delta in North America and one of the largest in the world. This river delta is also known as one of the most biologically diverse regions in the country.

Largest lake on an island

Baffin Island is not only Canada's largest island, but it's also home to the world's largest lake on an island. Measuring some 5,542 square km, Nettilling Lake is the largest lake in Nunavut and the 11th largest in Canada. It is located toward the island's south end, about 110 km southwest of Auyuittuq National Park. Covered by ice for most of the year, the lake is known to host only three fish species: Arctic char and two species of stickleback.

Second-largest glacier-fed lake

Located in Alberta's Jasper National Park, Maligne Lake is the second-largest glacier-fed lake in the world. The lake is 22 km long and 97 m deep.

Highest point of departure

It seems hard to believe, but there's a lake in central Ontario that's the highest freshwater lake in the Americas from which a skipper can circumnavigate the world by ocean-going vessel. At 265.5 m above sea level, Ontario's Balsam Lake is considered the "summit" of the Trent-Severn Waterway, a canal system that crosses Ontario's cottage country from Lake Ontario's Bay of Quinte to Lake Huron's Georgian Bay.

Largest freshwater delta

The globe's largest inland freshwater delta is found in Wood Buffalo National Park.

LAKE IN A LAKE

A lake in a lake? You bet. Ontario's Manitoulin Island is home to the world's largest lake on a freshwater island (and the world's largest lake in a lake, too). Lake Manitou has a surface area of approximately 104 square km. There are also a number of small islands on Manitou, making them islands on a lake on an island in a lake!

Salty lake

Water so buoyant it's impossible to sink? Head to the Dead Sea, right? Or go to central Saskatchewan's Little Manitou Lake. Fed by underground springs, the 13.3 square km lake has mineral salt concentrations of 180,000 mg per litre, making the water extremely buoyant.

Largest island in freshwater lake

The largest island in a freshwater lake in the world is Ontario's Manitoulin Island in Lake Huron. The 2,765 square km island is a continuation of the Bruce Peninsula, the strip of land stretching into Lake Huron that separates Georgian Bay from the larger area of the lake. The Bruce Peninsula is part of the Niagara Escarpment, a massive ridge of fossil-rich sedimentary rock that began to form 450 million years ago.

Southernmost island

Relatively speaking, it's an unassuming island in the middle of Lake Erie. But Middle Island is actually Canada's southernmost point. In 1999, the island was purchased by the Nature Conservancy of Canada to protect the Carolinian habitat and the rare and endangered species that call it home. In 2000, the island's ownership was transferred to Parks Canada, and Middle Island became part of Point Pelee National Park.

Largest island

With millions of lakes across the country and the longest coastline in the world, Canada is also home to thousands, if not millions, of islands. Most Canadians, however, are unlikely to ever see the nation's largest island, Nunavut's Baffin Island, which lies in the Arctic Ocean north of Labrador. At 507,451 square km, Baffin is also the fifth-largest island in the world. Nunavut's capital, Iqaluit, is located on the island's southern coast on Frobisher Bay.

Historic island

There are not too many places like this. Saint Croix Island, which lies on the United States' side of the St. Croix River, between Maine and New Brunswick, is recognized as a site of national historic significance to Canada. It is the location of the first attempt at French settlement in North America (1604). An international historic site and a national monument in the United States, there is an interpretation site for the island at Bayside, New Brunswick.

Largest freshwater archipelago

With all the country's fresh water, is it any wonder Canada is home to the world's largest freshwater archipelago? Ontario's 13,000 square km Georgian Bay, part of Lake Huron, is home to some 30,000 islands.

Island-lake-island-lake-island

Okay, follow closely: Canada is home to the world's largest island, in a lake, on an island, in a lake, on an island. About 120 km inland from the southern coast of Nunavut's portion of Victoria Island, the one-hectare, nameless island is found on a small lake that's on an island surrounded by a smaller lake.

LARGEST UNINHABITED ISLAND

Nunavut's Devon Island claims to be the largest island on Earth uninhabited by people. Located just north of Baffin Island, about one-third of Devon's 55,247 square km is covered by ice, while the rest of the island is largely barren.

Canada's 10 largest islands

1. Baffin Island, Nunavut 507,451 km^2
2. Victoria Island, Nunavut/Northwest Territories, 217,291 km^2
3. Ellesmere Island, Nunavut, 196,236 km^2
4. Newfoundland, 111,390 km^2
5. Banks Island, Northwest Territories, 70,028 km^2
6. Devon Island, Nunavut, 55,247 km^2
7. Axel Heiberg Island, Nunavut, 43, 178 km^2
8. Melville Island, Northwest Territories, 42,149 km^2
9. Southampton Island, Nunavut, 41, 214 km^2
10. Prince of Wales Island, Nunavut, 33,339 km^2

Eight out of 10 of Canada's largest islands are in Nunavut

Greenland

Nunavut

Northwest Territories

Quebec

Hudson Bay

Largest dune formation

Ontario's Sandbanks Provincial Park, on the shores of Lake Ontario near Picton, is home to the largest baymouth-barrier dune formation in the world. Some sections of the dune are 60 m high. The park's location and unique habitat make it a hot spot for migrating birds in the spring and fall.

Longest freshwater beach

That's a whole lotta sand! Ontario's Wasaga Beach is the longest freshwater beach in the world. It stretches 14 km along the shore of Lake Huron's Georgian Bay.

World's smallest desert

When you think of Canada, and when you think of the North, you naturally think of deserts — or maybe not! But Canada is home to what's called the world's smallest desert, the Carcross Desert in the Yukon. The area's dry climate and strong winds have created a small, 260-hectare series of sand dunes — but it's not technically a desert.

Largest dune fields

Think of long, sandy beaches and you probably don't think of Canada. You also probably don't think of Canada's north. But the Athabasca Sand Dunes, a series of dune fields running about 100 km along the south shore of Lake Athabasca in northwest Saskatchewan, is the largest active sand dune surface in Canada and one of the most northern dune fields on Earth.

First international peace park

Except for that war we won in 1812, Canada and the United States have had a relatively cordial relationship. Indeed, in 1932, the nations joined to create the world's first international peace park, Waterton-Glacier International Peace Park. (There are now 170 peace parks around the globe.) Designated a UNESCO world heritage site on December 6, 1995, the 4,556-square-km cross-border park joins Alberta's Waterton Lakes National Park and Montana's Glacier National Park.

Longest undefended border

Who says good fences make good neighbours? Since the War of 1812, Canada and the United States have shared the world's longest undefended border — 8,890 km. The border is marked on land by a 6-m wide, tree-free swath and 5,528 boundary monuments. There are also 2,457 reference monuments marking the water boundary.

First dark-sky preserve

Are you afraid of the dark? Then best to avoid the Torrance Barrens Conservation Area in Ontario's Muskoka region. The 1,902-hectare park was named the world's first permanent dark-sky preserve in 1999. Trees and bushes are stunted in height in this area of bedrock and wetlands, and hence Torrance Barrens offers sky watchers clear views of the night sky, with very little light pollution.

Largest dark-sky preserve

Wood Buffalo National Park (see next page) is the world's largest dark-sky preserve. The park was officially granted the dark-sky preserve designation in August 2013 by the Royal Astronomical Society of Canada for its work to preserve dark skies for the benefit of visitors and ecology.

LARGEST COUNTRY WITH SINGLE BORDER

Canada is the world's largest nation with only one land border with another country (the United States).

Largest provincial park

More than four times the size of Prince Edward Island, Quebec's Parc national Tursujuq is the largest provincial park in the country. The 26,107-square-km park, located on the eastern shore of Hudson Bay, was created on December 14, 2012.

First provincial park

The first provincial park in Canada was Queen Victoria Niagara Falls Park, which opened May 24, 1888 and lies near the famed falls themselves. Originally a 62.2-hectare park, the protected area has been expanded over the years to encompass 1,720 hectares along the Niagara River.

Largest national park

It seems fitting that Canada's largest national park (and the second-largest in the world) is named after North America's largest terrestrial animal. Wood Buffalo National Park, which straddles the Alberta-Northwest Territories border, spans 44,807 square km. It was established in 1992 to protect the last remaining herds of the continent's wood bison.

Largest mountain park

Looking for a park full of mountains? Look no further than Alberta's Jasper National Park, the largest mountain national park in the country. The 11,228-square-km park, boasts stunning mountain vistas, a plethora of wildlife and more than 1,200 kilometres of hiking trails.

First marine protected area

Canada's first federal marine protected area is considered to be Bird Rocks Migratory Bird Sanctuary. Located in the Gulf of St. Lawrence near the Magdalen Islands, the Bird Rocks and a one km zone around them (including the water) was established as a sanctuary in 1919.

FIRST ARCTIC NATIONAL PARK

The country's first national park north of the Arctic Circle is Nunavut's Auyuittuq National Park. Located on Baffin Island's Cumberland Peninsula, the 19,089-square-km park was created as a national park reserve in 1976 and became a national park in 2001, as part of the Nunavut Land Claims Agreement.

First national park

Canada's first national park, Banff National Park, was created in 1885, and was the world's third national park. The 6,641-square-km protected area in Alberta is the most-visited national park in the country.

First protected area

Montreal's Mount Royal Park is considered Canada's first protected area. It was inaugurated on Queen Victoria's birthday, May 24, in 1876.

First marine conservation area

Fathom Five National Marine Park was Canada's first national marine conservation area. Established in 1987, the park covers a 130-square-km area of water and 20 islands located off the end of Ontario's Bruce Peninsula, which separates Lake Huron from Georgian Bay. The park's waters are home to unique geology, plants, wildlife and 22 shipwrecks.

Slowest growing trees

The Niagara Escarpment, a ridge that runs east and west through south-central Ontario, is home to the world's slowest growing trees. Though the trees are the common eastern white cedar, the species grows particularly slowly in this environment, living up to 1,000 years.

Largest botanical garden

The Royal Botanical Gardens in Burlington, Ontario, is the largest botanical garden in Canada, with 1,100 hectares of gardens and nature reserves and more than 27 km of trails.

Oldest and longest footpath

The Bruce Trail, which runs from Niagara to Tobermory in Ontario along the Niagara Escarpment, is the nation's oldest and longest marked footpath. The trail stretches for 890 km, with another 400 km of associated trails.

Longest recreational trail

The Trans Canada Trail is the world's longest recreational trail. It is a 17,000 km network of close to 500 trails that runs across the country from the Atlantic to the Pacific oceans, connecting hundreds of communities. The trail, established in 1992, is still being expanded and will measure 24,000 km and go through every province and territory once completed.

Greenest city

It's nicknamed "Festival City" owing to its year-round slate of cultural events, but an equally apt moniker for Edmonton might be "City of Green." Alberta's capital lays claim to the largest urban green space in North America. The "Ribbon of Green" winds its way through the city along the shores of the North Saskatchewan River, with nature areas and more than 150 km of trails.

Most dinosaur fossils

Where will you find the richest area of dinosaur fossils in the world? Why, Alberta's Dinosaur Provincial Park, naturally. Since the 1880s, more than 150 complete dinosaur skeletons have been unearthed from a 27-km-area near the Red Deer River. More than 40 dinosaur species have been found here, as well as the fossils of 450 other organisms.

First Canadian atlas

In 1906, the first edition of the *Atlas of Canada* was published by the federal Department of the Interior. It was one of the first national atlases in the world. At the time, Canada's population was seven million. Thirty percent of the people lived in 15 towns and cities with populations of more than 25,000. The sixth edition, published online in 1999, was one of the world's first online atlases.

Southernmost land

While Middle Island in Lake Erie is Canada's most southerly piece of land, Point Pelee is the most southerly tip of Canada's main land mass. Stretching out into Lake Erie, the point is home to Point Pelee National Park and a major migration stopover for numerous bird species. Indeed, 42 of 52 regularly occurring warbler species have been spotted at Pelee.

Closest to centre

At a latitude of 50°26' and a longitude of 104°37', Regina is the Canadian city closest to the geographical centre of North America.

Longest place names

Sympathies if one these place names, the nation's longest, is in your address.

	Place name	Type	Province	Characters
1.	Dysart, Dudley, Harcourt, Guilford, Harburn, Bruton, Havelock, Eyre and Clyde	Township municipality	ON	68
2.	Cape St. George-Petit Jardin-Grand Jardin-De Grau-Marches Point-Loretto	Community	NFD	65
3.	L'Annonciation-de-la-Bienheureuse-Vierge-Marie-de-Nazareth	Geographical area	QC	58
4.	Stanley Bridge, Hope River, Bayview, Cavendish and North Rustico	Village	PEI	56
5.	L'Immaculée-Conception -de-la-Bienheureuse-Vierge-Marie	Geographical area	QC	54
6.	Cours d'eau du Cordon des Terres des Sixième et Septième Rangs	Stream	QC	52
7.	Cours d'eau de la Concession Sud-Est du Rang Saint-David	Stream	QC	48
8.	Décharge des Neuvième Dixième et Onzième Concessions	Stream	QC	46
9.	Lower North Branch Little Southwest Miramichi River Embranchement des Rangs Saint-Georges et Séraphine (tie)	Stream Stream	NB QC	45
10.	Cours d'eau des Cinquième et Sixième Rangs de Milton	Stream	QC	44

Northernmost land

Cape Columbia, Nunavut, is Canada's most northerly point of land.

Northernmost point of North America

It's certainly aptly named. Zenith Point, Nunavut, is the northern-most point of continental North America.

Westernmost point

Canada's westernmost point is Boundary Peak in the Yukon, along the Yukon-Alaska border.

Westernmost community

The nation's most westerly community is the Yukon's Beaver Creek. Located on the Alaska Highway at the 141st meridian, the community is home to the White River First Nations and considered to be Canada's gateway to Alaska.

Easternmost point

The most easterly point in Canada and North America is Cape Spear, Newfoundland.

Easternmost point of North America

The most easterly point of continental North America is Cape St. Charles, Labrador.

Northernmost community

Grise Fiord, Nunavut, lays claim to the title of most northerly community in North America. Only about 150 people, mostly Inuit, live in the hamlet, which was established in 1953 when the federal government relocated Inuit families from northern Quebec and northern Baffin Island to this spot to strengthen Canadian claims to the High Arctic.

Northernmost inhabited place

Alert, Nunavut, at latitude 82° 30' N, is the world's northernmost permanently inhabited place. Located on the northeastern coast of Ellesmere Island on the Lincoln Sea, Alert is the site of an Environment Canada weather station, an atmosphere observatory and a military station, which is occupied year-round by an unknown number of personnel. The settlement experiences 106 days of full darkness each year, and an average annual temperature of −18°C.

Most densely populated

Despite being Canada's smallest province, Prince Edward Island is the nation's most densely populated. It's estimated there are 23.9 individuals per square km on the island.

Hydrographic apex

The hydrographic apex of North America — the only spot on the continent where water flows to three different oceans from one point — is the Columbia Icefield in Alberta's Jasper National Park.

First people in North America

The earliest known signs of humans in North America have been found in the Yukon's Bluefish Caves. Butchered mammoth bones and primitive tools were discovered that date to 15,000 and 12,000 years ago and evidence suggests these peoples migrated from Asia. The tools are made with a stone technology reminiscent of the Dyuktai culture of Siberia.

Most petroglyphs and pictographs

Alberta's Writing-on-Stone Provincial Park, located in the southeast corner of the province, is home to the largest concentration of First Nation petroglyphs (rock carvings) and pictographs (rock paintings) on the great plains of North America.

First capital

The first capital of Upper Canada (present-day Ontario) was Newark, now Niagara-on-the-Lake. It was changed to York (present-day Toronto) in 1793 to protect it from American attack.

Oldest European funeral mound

Newfoundland is home to the oldest known funeral mound on the continent, the burial site of a child that dates to approximately 7,500 years ago.

Highest Arctic land area

Canada's Arctic Archipelago is the largest high-Arctic land area in the world, apart from Greenland (which is almost entirely covered in ice and geologically part of the archipelago). The chain is made up of 94 islands larger than 130 square km and 36,469 smaller islands. It has six of the world's 30 largest islands.

Earliest settlement

The earliest known human settlement in Canada is found on British Columbia's Haida Gwaii. It is estimated that an archeological site at Nanu was inhabited between 15,000 and 12,000 years ago. Stone tools and remains of large butchered animals have been found at the site, which is thought to be the longest continuously occupied settlement in Canada.

Head-Smashed-In Buffalo Jump
Interpretive Centre

Hours of Operation: Open 9 a.m. to 6 p.m.

Alberta
COMMUNITY DEVELOPMENT

Best buffalo jump

Talk about a literal place name! Alberta's Head-Smashed-In Buffalo Jump is considered one of the Earth's oldest, largest and best-preserved buffalo jumps. Now a UNESCO world heritage site, the spot was used by Aboriginal peoples for close to 6,000 years to drive plains bison to their deaths by stampeding them off the edge of the cliffs.

NON-GEOGRAPHIC BOUNDARIES

Saskatchewan is the only province in the country that has no geographical features as boundaries.

ONLY BILINGUAL PROVINCE

The nation's only officially bilingual province? New Brunswick, where about 33 percent of people speak French.

Most impressive waterfalls

It's been said Ontario's famous Niagara Falls are the world's largest by volume. However, that is simply not true. They may be the globe's most impressive, but they rank 11th on Earth by volume, with more than 168,000 cubic m of water going over the edge every minute. The falls have moved back 11 km in 12,500 years, due to erosion, and may be world's fastest moving waterfalls.

Highest waterfalls

When it comes to waterfalls, much debate surrounds the question of which are the tallest. After all, many of them fall in a series of cascades, so where to start and end when measuring them is often a matter of discussion. Here's the list of the 10 highest waterfalls in Canada from worldwaterfalldatabase.com. All of them are in British Columbia.

James Bruce Falls 840 m	Gold Creek Falls 610 m	Unnamed waterfall 610 m	Unnamed waterfall 610 m	Lady Peak Falls 600 m	Madden Falls 579 m	Rugged Glacier Falls 560 m	Daniels River Falls 540 m	Swiftcurrent Falls 537 m	Marion Falls 527 m

"Great" Canadian places

These are literally "Great" Canadian places:

- Great Barachois Lake, NS
- Great Barasway Lookout, NL
- Great Barasway Pond, NL
- Great Barren Lake, NS
- Great Bear Lake, NT
- Great Bear River, NT
- Great Bear Creek, BC
- Great Beaver Lake, BC
- Great Black Island, NL
- Great Brook, NL
- Great Burnt Island, NL
- Great Buse, NL
- Great Calf Island, NS
- Great Chain Island, BC
- Great Coat Island, NL
- Great Colinet Island, NL
- Great Cormorandier Island, NL
- Great Denier Island, NL
- Great Duck Island, NB
- Great Duck Island, ON
- Great Eastern Pond, NL
- Great Falls, NS
- Great Falls, MB
- Great French Beach, NL
- Great Gulch River, NL
- Great Gull Lake, NL
- Great Gull River, NL
- Great Hill, NS
- Great Island, NL
- Great Island, NS
- Great Island, Manitoba
- Great Jervis Island, NL
- Great La Cloche Island, ON
- Great Lake, ON
- Great Manitou Island, ON
- Great Mountain, NL
- Great Mountain Lake, ON
- Great Northern Mountain, NL
- Great Pike Lake, ON
- Great Pine Lake, NS
- Great Pond, NL
- Great Pond, NB
- Great Portage Lake, ON
- Great Pubnico Lake, NS
- Great Rattling Brook, NL
- Great Ridge, NS
- Great Rock Peak, BC
- Great Sacred Island, NL
- Great Sand Hills, SK
- Great Seal Island, NL
- Great Slave Lake, NT
- Great Snow Mountain, BC
- Great Thrum, NS
- Great Tinker Island, NL
- Great Verdon Island, NL
- Great Village River, NS
- Great West Ridge, AB

Wettest spot

Bring an umbrella (1). Mitchell Inlet on British Columbia's Haida Gwaii Island is Canada's wettest place. It receives 6,325 ml of precipitation each year, of which 99 percent is rain. That's more than 6 m annually!

Wettest city

Bring an umbrella (2). Prince Rupert, British Columbia, is Canada's wettest city. It gets an average of 2,500 ml of precipitation every year.

Wettest community

Canada's rainiest community is Klemtu, British Columbia. Four hundred and sixty people live in Klemtu, located on Swindle Island on the Pacific coast. The nearest Environment Canada weather station receives 5,047 ml of precipitation annually, most of which is rain.

Most expensive floods

It's still fresh in the memory of most Canadians and certainly in the minds of southern Albertans. The Insurance Bureau of Canada has called the floods that hit the southern area of the province from June 20 to June 24, 2013, the costliest insured natural disaster in Canada. Property damages from the flooding were estimated at more than $1.7 billion dollars.

Rain in the rainiest province

British Columbia certainly lives up to its reputation as a rainy province. Here's a chart showing the average annual precipitation for the province's wettest communities.

Days	Place	inches	ml
205	Hartley Bay	184.0	4673
169	Tahsis	169.5	4305
207	Port Renfrew	138.0	3505
225	Port Alice	134.9	3427
206	Ucluelet	131.9	3351
208	Tofino	128.8	3271
229	Prince Rupert	120.5	3060

Wettest places outside BC

The rest of Canada hardly compares to British Columbia when it comes to annual precipitation averages. The next wettest community receives 65 fewer rainy days and more than 1,000 ml less precipitation. Here are the nation's other wettest places:

Average total yearly precipitation

Days	Place	inches	ml
164	Wreck Cove Brook, NS	76.6	1946
183	Red Harbour, NL	72.5	1841
147	Pool's Cove, NL	72.0	1828
154	Guysborough, NS	71.4	1815
219	Forêt Montmorency, QC	62.3	1583
236	St-Fortunat, QC	60.7	1542
172	Alma, NB	59.5	1510
163	Allenford, ON	50.9	1294
175	New Glasgow, PEI	49.5	1258
149	Blyth, ON	49.1	1247
162	Waterton Village, AB	43.2	1096

Most consecutive rainy days

Vancouver claims the record among large Canadian cities (those with a population of 100,000 and greater) for the most consecutive days of rain: 29, in 1953, between January 6 to February 3. The city nearly broke the record in January 2006, after 23 straight days of rain.

Rainiest days on record

Amount of precipitation in one day

Date	Place	inches	ml
January 26, 1984	McInnes Island, BC	12.6	319
January 14, 1961	Seymour Falls, BC	12.4	314
November 14, 1991	Mitchell Inlet, BC	12.1	306
November 11, 1990	Tahsis, BC	11.8	300
November 10, 1990	Seymour Falls, BC	11.8	300

Most rain in one day

The greatest recorded one-day rainfall in Canada occurred October 6, 1967, at Ucluelet Brynnor Mines, British Columbia. A total of 489.2 ml (nearly half a litre) of rain fell.

Coldest city

Canada's coldest city? A tie between Saskatoon and Regina (pictured here), with –50°C recorded on February 1, 1893, and January 1, 1885, respectively. The most recent sub –40°C temperature recorded in a Canadian city? Sherbrooke, Quebec, at –41.2°C on January 15, 2004.

Coldest wind chill

Canadians know that frigid temperatures are one thing, but wind chill is another. The nation's record wind chill was set on January 28, 1989, at Pelly Bay, Northwest Territories. The temperature was a nippy –51°C. The wind chill? A super-frosty –91°C!

Coldest big city

Saskatoon holds the record for the coldest major Canadian city, based on mean daily temperature (averaged over the year), at 2.2°C. Winterpeg, er, Winnipeg, is actually the third coldest major city at 2.6°C, following Saguenay, Quebec, at 2.3°C.

Coldest major cities

Canada's coldest major cities in winter, based on daily average temperature in December, January and February:

City	Daily Average °C
Winnipeg	–15.3
Saskatoon	–14.8
Saguenay	–13.9
Regina	–13.8
Sudbury	–11.5
Quebec	–11.0
Sherbrooke	–10.1

Coldest year

It seems fair to call it Canada's coldest year: in 1972, every weather-reporting station in the country reported annual temperatures below average, the only time on record this ever happened.

Cold in 1947

1947 was a particularly cool year in northwestern Canada. Check out these other Canadian low temperature records:

Location	°C	Date
Mayo, YT	–62.2	February 3, 1947
Watson Lake, YT	–58.9	January 31, 1947
Norman Wells, NWT	–54.4	February 4, 1947
Whitehorse, YT	–52.2	January 31, 1947
Fort Nelson, BC	–51.7	January 30, 1947
Dease Lake, BC	–51.2	January 31, 1947
Yellowknife, NWT	–51.2	January 31, 1947
Fort McMurray, AB	–50.6	February 1, 1947

Lowest temperature

Brrr. The lowest temperature ever recorded in Canada and North America? The village of Snag, Yukon, registered –63°C on February 3, 1947.

Most lightning

Flash! The north shore of Lake Erie near Highgate, Ontario, gets the greatest annual number of days (50 in 2006) with lightning of any inland place in Canada. Pictured here: Lightning strikes the CN Tower in Toronto.

Most lightning in one year

Call it Canada's lightning capital. Windsor, Ontario, is the Canadian city that had the most lightning in any one year: 47 days with lightning in 2007.

Northernmost lightning

The farthest north a lightning flash was detected in Canada over the eastern Beaufort Sea, north of Tuktoyatuk, Northwest Territories on August 11, 2013.

Coldest places

Canada's other coldest places:

Location	°C	Date
Old Crow, YT	−59.4	January 5, 1975
Iroquois Falls, ON	−58.3	January 23, 1935
Shepherd Bay, NWT	−57.8	February 13, 1973
Inukik, NWT	−56.7	February 4, 1968
Prince Albert, SK	−56.7	February 1, 1893
Dawson, YT	−55.8	February 11, 1979
Eureka, NU	−55.3	February 15, 1979

COLDEST TEMPERATURES IN SOUTHERN CANADA

And the coldest recorded temperatures in southern Canada:

Location	°C	Date
Norway House, MB	−52.8	January 9, 1899
Esker 2, NL	−51.1	February 17, 1973
Schefferville, QC	−50.6	February 7, 1950
Sisson Dam, NB	−47.2	February 1, 1955
Upper Stewiacke, NS	−41.1	January 31, 1920
Kilmahumaig, PEI	−37.2	January 26, 1884

Canada is pretty cool

Canada is just about the coolest country—literally. It vies with Russia for first place as the coldest nation in the world, with an average daily annual temperature of −5.6°C.

Biggest snowfall in one year

The heaviest annual snowfall the country has witnessed was in the Revelstoke-Mount Copeland area of British Columbia. The region spent the winter of 1971–72 digging out from a total of 2,446.5 cm, or nearly 24.5 m of snow.

Biggest snowfall

Get the shovel, er, shovels! The greatest single-day snowfall recorded in Canada was February 11, 1999, when Tahtsa, British Columbia, was blanketed with nearly a metre and a half of the white stuff (145 cm, to be exact). That broke a record of 118.1 cm of snow that fell on Lakelse Lake, British Columbia, on January 17, 1974. Neither is near the world record of 192 cm, set at Silver Lake, Colorado, on April 15, 1921.

Killing cold

Deadly cold. More Canadians die each year from exposure to extreme cold temperatures than from other natural events, according to Statistics Canada. An average of 108 people die annually from the cold, while only 17 succumb to other nature-related events.

Community with the highest snowfall

A snow blower must be standard equipment for a homeowner in Woody Point, Newfoundland. Located on Bonne Bay on the province's west coast, Woody Point is the Canadian community that receives the highest recorded average snowfall. Over 89 days, 638 cm of snow falls each year.

HIGHEST AVERAGE SNOWFALL

The highest average annual snowfall ever recorded at an Environment Canada weather station is 1,388 cm on Mount Fidelity, British Columbia. This mountain in Glacier National Park averages 141 days of snow a year.

Winterpeg

Turns out Winnipeg may still have a legitimate claim to that Winterpeg moniker. Of Canada's large cities, the 'Peg leads when it comes to the average number of days when the temperature doesn't break 0°C, at 117. Perhaps it's not surprising that Saskatoon and Saguenay, Quebec, are second and third in the same category, with 112 and 110 days, respectively.

Highest average snowfalls

Canada's highest recorded average annual snowfalls:

Days	Place	inches	cm
141	Mount Fidelity, Glacier National Park, BC	546.4	1388.0
114	Unuk River, Eskay Creek Mine, BC	511.3	1298.6
104	Tahtsa Lake West, BC	384.1	975.7
78	Grouse Mountain, North Vancouver, BC	342.0	868.7
112	Rogers Pass, BC	340.4	864.7
78	Pleasant Camp, BC	285.0	723.8
90	Fraser Camp, BC	276.8	703.2
69	Hollyburn Ridge, West Vancouver, BC	257.7	654.6

Snowiest communities

Canada's snowiest communities based on average annual snowfall records.

Days	Place	inches	cm
89	Woody Point, NL	251.1	637.9
117	Forêt Montmorency, QC	244.1	619.9
125	Cape Dyer, NU	218.2	554.2
85	Murdochville, QC	215.7	547.8
103	St. Anthony, NL	214.0	543.7
51	Main Brook, NL	202.8	515.0

Snowiest cities

When it comes to snow in Canada's largest cities, 10 of them receive an average of more than 2 m of the white stuff annually (based on urban centres with more than 100,000 population in 2011 and snow data averages between 1981 and 2010).

Annual average snowfall a year:

City	inches	cm
St. John's, NL	131.9	335.0
Saguenay, QC	126.6	321.7
Quebec City, QC	119.4	303.4
Sherbrooke, QC	112.8	286.5
Moncton, NB	111.0	282.0
Sudbury, ON	103.7	263.4
Trois-Rivières, QC	102.0	259.0
St. John, NB	94.3	239.6
Barrie, ON	87.8	223.0
Montreal, QC	82.5	209.5

Biggest blizzards

Canada's biggest blizzards, based on biggest single-day snowfalls on record:

Date	Place	inches	cm
February 11, 1999	Tahtsa Lake West, BC	57.1	145.0
December 4, 1985	Pleasant Camp, BC	50.0	127.0
March 20, 1885	Cap-de-la-Madeleine, QC	48.0	121.9
January 17, 1974	Lakelse Lake, BC	46.5	118.0
February 11, 1999	Terrace, BC	44.6	113.4
February 18, 1972	Kitimat, BC	44.2	112.3
January 16, 1976	Stewart, BC	41.6	105.7
February 5, 1988	Main Brook, NL	41.3	105.0
January 11, 1968	Kemano, BC	41.0	104.1
January 27, 2000	Unuk River, Eskay Creek Mine, BC	40.9	104.0
January 6, 1988	Nain, NL	40.7	103.4
February 17, 1943	Colinet, BC	40.0	101.6

Largest snow-removal budget

Winter and snow are no strangers to those living in the city of Montreal. Indeed, so much snow hits the city — an average of 2 m a year — that it has the largest snow-removal budget of any metropolis in the world. For the winter of 2011–12, the average cost of snow removal for a snowfall of at least 20 cm was $17 million. On December 27, 2012, the city had its largest recorded one-day snowfall: 45 cm.

Longest-lasting snowfalls

Outside of Canada's territories, here are the places with the highest number of average days each year with at least one cm of snow on the ground:

Location	Days
Mt. Fidelity, Glacier National Park, BC	271
Inukjuak, QC	228
Schefferville, QC	221
Churchill Falls, NL	221
Tahtsa Lake West, BC	216
Churchill, MB	215
Rogers Pass, BC	215
Unuk River, Eskay Creek, BC	212
Makkovik, NL	210
Nain, NL	205
Wabush Lake, NL	202
Kuujjuaq, QC	201
Poste Montagnais, QC	200

Montreal's worst snowstorm

Montreal gets a lot of snow (see bottom left). The worst snowstorm to hit the city happened on March 4, 1971. In total, 47 cm of snow hit the city, and 110 km per hour winds created snow drifts as high as two storeys. The storm created power outages that lasted up to 10 days in some areas, and 17 people died as a result of the blizzard.

Longest-lasting snowfall

Places in Canada's south typically see more snow, but it lasts longer in the country's north. Indeed, the nation's northernmost settlement, Alert, Nunavut, is covered in snow for longer each year on average than anywhere else — at least one cm of snow covers the ground for an average 304 days annually.

Highest frequency of snow

There's quantity of snow, then there's frequency. The following big Canadian cities had the highest average number of days with at least 2 mm or more snow.

Saguenay, Quebec	93
St. John's, NL	79
Sherbrooke, QC	76
Sudbury, ON	75
Quebec City, QC	70
Thunder Bay, ON	62
Kitchener–Waterloo, ON	62
London, ON	60
Montreal, QC	59
Regina, SK	56

Snowiest May

At an average of 54 days with at least 2 mm of snow, Calgary, Alberta, just barely doesn't make the list on the right as one of the country's biggest cities with most days of fresh snow. That said, it receives more snow in May, September and October than any other Canadian city. On average, Calgary has two to three days of snow in May, one or two in September and four (!) in October.

Most months of snow

Snow, snow, go away. Ten of the nation's largest cities have at least 1 cm of snow on the ground for at least three months (or more than 120 days).

Average number of days a year when snow is 1 cm or more deep:

	City	Days
1.	Saguenay, Quebec	155
2.	Quebec City, Quebec	141
3.	Sudbury, Ontario	136
4.	Trois-Rivières, Quebec	134
5.	Sherbrooke, Quebec	133
6.	Edmonton, Alberta	133
7.	Winnipeg, Manitoba	128
8.	Thunder Bay, Ontario	126
9.	Regina, Saskatchewan	125
10.	Saskatoon, Saskatchewan	124

Major cities with the least snow

Here are the least snowiest major cities in the country, outside of British Columbia.

Annual average snowfall a year:

City	inches	cm
Saskatoon, SK	28.9	73.4
Brantford, ON	38.7	98.4
Regina, SK	39.4	100.2
Oshawa, ON	41.6	105.8
Winnipeg, MB	44.8	113.7
Hamilton, ON	46.5	118.1

City with the least snow

So, do you want to live in a big Canadian city and avoid the snow? Victoria is the place for you. The capital of British Columbia receives only 33 cm of snowfall each year on average, and it lands over just 7 days. The snow doesn't last long either. On average, accumulated snow is higher than 1 cm for just 5 days each year.

Three cities with the least snow

Of course, if you want to miss the snow, three of British Columbia's other major cities—Vancouver, Abbotsford and Kelowna—are also good bets, and rank second, third and fourth, respectively, as the nation's least snowiest. Vancouver gets just 44.6 cm of snow on average each year, Abbotsford sees an average of 55.2 cm annually, and Kelowna gets 63.5 cm.

Cities with the least frequency of snow

Perhaps not surprisingly, many of the nation's least snowy cities also don't see snow very often. Here are the Canadian cities that get at least two millimeters of new snow for the fewest number of days, on average, each year:

City	Days
Victoria, BC	7
Vancouver, BC	9
Abbotsford, BC	12
Kelowna, BC	21
Brantford, ON	24
Halifax, NS	25
Oshawa, ON	27
Saskatoon, SK	28
Peterborough, ON	34
Hamilton, ON	36

FEWEST DAYS WITH SNOW

Don't like a white Christmas? Try one of these cities, which have the fewest average days each year with 1 cm or more of snow.

City	Days
Victoria, British Columbia	5
Vancouver, British Columbia	9
Abbotsford, British Columbia	13
Kelowna, British Columbia	50
Windsor, Ontario	53
Halifax, Nova Scotia	54
St. Catharines, Ontario	56
Oshawa, Ontario	63
Toronto, Ontario	65
Hamilton, Ontario	74

Ice storm of the century

Some called it "the storm of the century." Whatever you consider it, the ice storm that hit Quebec and Ontario starting on January 5, 1998, was the costliest winter storm in Canadian history. According to the Insurance Bureau of Canada, the six days of freezing rain led to month-long power outages in some locations and a total of $2 billion (in 2011 dollars) in insured losses.

Toronto's worst snowfall

There was that time Toronto called in the army (early January 1999), but the worst single-day snowfall in the country's largest city was actually December 11, 1944. The winter storm dropped 48 cm of snow on Toronto. It was accompanied by gale-force winds that created huge snowdrifts. In all, 57.2 cm of snow fell over two days, and 21 people died, including 13 from overexertion.

Toronto's snowiest January

Lest Toronto get too bad a rap for calling in the army, the series of snowstorms that struck the city in January 1999 hit the city with almost a year's worth of snow in two weeks, from the 2nd to the 15th. In total, it was the snowiest January in the city's history, with 118.4 cm of snow and the most snow on the ground at one time, at 65 cm.

Highest average temperature

Canada's West Coast is well known for being rainy, but not for being hot. Still, you could consider Victoria Canada's hottest major city. It has the country's highest recorded average daily maximum temperature at 15.3°C. Victoria also has the hottest recorded nights, with an average daily minimum temperature of 7.1°C.

Hot day in Saskatchewan

On July 5, 1937, the mercury soared to 45°C in Yellow Grass, Saskatchewan.

CITIES WITH THE HIGHEST AVERAGE TEMPERATURES

Canadian cities with the highest recorded average daily maximum temperature annually:

City	High °F	High °C
Victoria, BC	60	15.3
Abbotsford, BC	59	15.1
Kelowna, BC	59	14.7
Windsor, ON	58	14.4
Vancouver, BC	57	13.9
St. Catharines, ON	56	13.6
Brantford, ON	56	13.2
Hamilton, ON	56	13.1
Toronto, ON	55	12.9
London, ON	55	12.7
Oshawa, ON	54	12.1

Hottest cities

Canadian cities with more than 10 days a year where the temperature reaches at least 30°C or higher:

City	Days
Kelowna, BC	26
Windsor, ON	23
Hamilton, ON	18
Regina, SK	16
St. Catharines, ON	14
Winnipeg, MB	13
Saskatoon, SK	13
Brantford, ON	13
Ottawa, ON	12
Toronto, ON	12

Temperatures higher than 40°C

Here's a list of when and where temperatures 40°C and higher were recorded in Canada:

Location	°C	Day
Midale and Yellow Grass, SK	45.0	July 5, 1937
Lillooet and Lytton, BC	44.4	July 16 & 17, 1941
St Albans, MB	44.4	July 11, 1936
Emerson, MB	44.4	July 12, 1936
Brandon and Morden, MB	43.3	July 11, 1936
Regina, SK	43.3	July 5, 1937
Fort Macleod, AB	43.3	July 18, 1941
Oliver, BC	42.8	July 27, 1939
Osoyoos, BC	42.8	July 27, 1998
Spences Bridge, BC	42.5	July 23, 1994
Medicine Hat, AB	42.2	July 12, 1886
Moose Jaw, SK	41.7	August 6, 1949
Winnipeg, MB	40.6	August 7, 1949
Saskatoon, SK	40.6	June 5, 1988
Kamloops, BC	40.6	July 31, 1971
Atikokan, ON	42.2	July 11 & 12, 1936
Northwest River, NL	41.7	August 11, 1914
Windsor, ON	40.2	June 25, 1988
Temiscamingue, QC	40.0	July 6, 1921

HOTTEST YEAR

The hottest year: 1998. Canada recorded its second warmest winter and warmest spring, summer and fall. Temperatures that year were an average 2.4°C higher than typical.

Longest growing seasons

Canadian cities with the longest growing seasons based on the average number of frost-free days:

City	Days
Vancouver, BC	237
Victoria, BC	211
Abbotsford, BC	208
Toronto, ON	203
Windsor, ON	195
Halifax, NS	182
St. Catharines, ON	179
Hamilton, ON	177
Oshawa, ON	168
Peterborough, ON	168

Hottest cities at night

The country's hottest cities at night, based on average daily minimum temperature annually:

City	Low °F	Low °C
Victoria, BC	45	7.1
Vancouver, BC	44	6.8
Toronto, ON	43	5.9
Abbotsford, BC	42	5.8
Windsor, ON	42	5.4
St. Catharines, ON	40	4.4
Kelowna, BC	39	4.1
Oshawa, ON	39	4.1
Hamilton, ON	39	4.0
Halifax, NS	38	3.6

Rainiest, foggiest, windiest

Cold, foggy and windy. Sounds like St. John's? Okay, it may be an unfair generalization, but of all Canadian cities, St. John's has the most days per year with freezing rain (38) and fog (121), and the most wind (an average annual wind speed of 24 km per hour).

Foggiest place in the world

The Grand Banks off Newfoundland is considered the foggiest place in the world. The area experiences 40 percent fog cover in the winter and up to 84 percent in the summer.

Cold summers

It could claim the title of "bad summer capital of Canada." St. John's has the nation's lowest average daily summer temperature (at just 13.9°C) and the fewest hot days (an average of only 0.2 days during June, July and August when the temperature exceeds 30°C.). Vancouver could be considered a close second for that ominous title. It has a daily average summer temperature of 16.8°C and 0.2 days of summer temperatures over 30°C.

Freezing cities in summer

Yes, it happens. Below zero temperatures in summer—yes, summer—in large Canadian cities. Here are the seven cities across the country that have seen the freezing mark in June, July or August:

City	Lowest °C	Date
Regina, SK	−5.6	June 12, 1969
Calgary, AB	−3.3	June 8, 1891
Saskatoon, SK	−3.3	June 9, 1903
Winnipeg, MB	−3.3	June 3, 1964
St. John's, NL	−3.3	June 1, 1970
Sherbrooke, QC	−2.2	June 3, 1965
Saguenay, QC	−2.2	June 12, 1946

DRIEST YEAR

The driest year ever recorded in Canada occurred in 1949 at Arctic Bay, Northwest Territories, where only 12.7 ml of precipitation fell.

Most winter sunshine

Winnipeg has more hours of winter sunshine than any other Canadian city.

Deadliest heat wave

Environment Canada calls it the "deadliest heat wave in history." From July 5 to 17, 1936, temperatures in Manitoba and Ontario were more than 44°C and responsible for the death of 1,180 people (largely infants and the elderly). In an unfortunate twist of fate, 400 of those deaths were attributed to drowning from people trying to escape the heat. It was so hot that steel railways and bridge girders twisted, and crops dried up.

Most sunshine ever

"Get out the suntan lotion," isn't a commonly heard refrain in Canada's Far North. But the most sunshine any community in Canada ever observed in one month was 621 hours in Eureka, Ellesmere Island, Northwester Territories, during May 1973. SPF 50, anyone?

Sunniest big city

Looking for a staycation suntan? Move to Calgary. It is the nation's sunniest large city, getting 2,396 hours of sunshine on average annually. And it comes over 333 days. That's more than half of the city's daylight hours.

Sunshine capital

Estevan, Canada's sunshine capital is in southeast Saskatchewan. It averages 2,540 hours of sunlight each year.

Driest city in Canada

Conserve the water. Medicine Hat, Alberta, has more dry days than any other Canadian city, with 271 days per year without measurable precipitation.

Calmest city

Don't go fly a kite — at least not in Kelowna, British Columbia; because chances are slim you'll have enough wind for liftoff. Kelowna is Canada's least windy city, with 39 percent of wind observations per year indicating calm conditions.

WINDIEST DAY

This was one windy day: on November 18, 1931, in Cape Hopes Advance, Quebec, the nation's highest recorded hourly wind speed, was set at 201.1 km per hour.

Most hours of sunshine

Despite the fact they're some of the country's snowiest and coldest cities, the following cities are also the sunniest. Here's the list of the nine cities (after Number One: Calgary) that received the highest average hours of sunlight annually:

City	Hours
Winnipeg, MB	2,353
Edmonton, AB	2,345
Regina, SK	2,318
Saskatoon, SK	2,268
Thunder Bay, ON	2,121
Hamilton, ON	2,111
Victoria, BC	2,109
Ottawa, ON	2,084
Toronto, ON	2,066

Most days of sunshine

Here's the nation's top ten sunniest cities, as measured by average days where the sun shines brightly enough to be measured:

City	Days
Calgary, AB	333
Edmonton, AB	325
Regina, SK	322
Saskatoon, SK	319
Winnipeg, MB	316
Victoria, BC	308
Montreal, QC	305
Toronto, ON	305
Thunder Bay, ON	305
Kelowna, BC	304

Percentage of sunshine

Here's a list of the country's sunniest cities, as measured by the percentage of the daylight hours the sun shines on average:

City	% sunshine
Calgary, AB	52
Winnipeg, MB	51
Edmonton, AB	50
Regina, SK	50
Saskatoon, SK	49
Thunder Bay, ON	46
Hamilton, ON	45
Ottawa, ON	45
Toronto, ON	44
Montreal, QC	44

Warming country

All of Canada has become warmer since the mid-20th century. Between 1948 and 2007, the nation's average temperature rose by 1.4°C.

Fastest rising temperatures

Need proof that climate change is a problem? Average winter temperatures in the Yukon and northern British Columbia went up by 4.9°C between 1948 and 2007 — the fastest rising temperatures in the country.

Biggest mercury jump

There's a saying in Canada that if you don't like the weather, wait five minutes. Never could that have been truer than in Pincher Creek, Alberta, where Canada's most extreme temperature change was recorded. The mercury soared from –19°C to 22°C in just one hour.

The hottest and the coldest

As most Canadians know and have experienced, this country can deliver a wide range of temperatures, from cold winter nights to hot summer days. Interestingly, among Canada's large cities, Regina lays claim to both the country's lowest recorded temperature and its highest. The city sweltered at 43.3°C on July 5, 1937. Likewise, Winnipeg and Saskatoon, both holding cold-weather records themselves, also posted some of the highest recorded temperatures for large Canadian cities; they tied for second place at 40.6°C (Winnipeg on August 7, 1949 and Saskatoon on June 5, 1988).

No change in fall temperatures

Two parts of the country have bucked the warming trend. During autumn in the extreme south of Ontario and Quebec, the average temperature has not changed since 1948.

PROVINCES GETTING COLDER

Other places in Canada have also seen average seasonal temperatures that don't follow the overall warming trend. Since 1948, the Atlantic provinces have grown colder in winter, and in the months of September, October and November, average temperatures decreased in Alberta, Saskatchewan, Manitoba, the Yukon and northern British Columbia.

Windiest place

Hold onto your hat! Cap St. James, located at the south end of Haida Gwaii, British Columbia, is Canada's windiest place. It sees more days with gale-force winds than anywhere else in the nation.

Longest tracked tornado

It was a deadly and disastrous day on May 31, 1985, when a total of 14 tornadoes hit a number of Ontario communities, including Barrie (pictured here), Grand Valley, Orangeville and Tottenham. The storms killed 12 people and damaged more than 1,000 buildings. Of particular note was the Grand Valley tornado, which started near Arthur and travelled east to Campbellford. It is considered one of the longest tracked tornadoes in Canada, wrecking havoc over 115 km.

Deadliest tornado

Known as the "Regina Cyclone," the tornado that hit Saskatchewan's capital in the late afternoon of June 30, 1912, is considered the deadliest such storm in Canadian history. The whirlwind tore through six city blocks, killed some 40 people and injured 300 more. It destroyed 500 buildings and left a quarter of the city's population homeless. It took an estimated 46 years to pay for the damages of the three-minute storm.

Cities ranked by climate

Here is the Climate Severity Index for select Canadian major cities: (see top right)

Victoria	15
Vancouver	19
Calgary	35
Toronto	36
Edmonton	37
Fredericton	41
Saskatoon	42
Montreal	43
Ottawa	44
Whitehorse	46
Halifax	47
Charlottetown	48
Saint John	48
Regina	49
Winnipeg	51
Quebec City	53
Yellowknife	57
St. John's	56

Famous Shipwreck

Immortalized in singer Gordon Lightfoot's song "The Wreck of the Edmund Fitzgerald," a severe storm on November 10, 1975 — accompanied by 20 m high waves on Lake Superior — sank the largest bulk ore carrier on the Great Lakes, the *Edmund Fitzgerald*. The ship's crew of 29 was lost.

City with the worst climate

Based on the Climate Severity Index, developed by Environment Canada to rate an area's climate based on human comfort and well being, St. John's is the major Canadian city with the worst climate. The city scores 56 out of 100 on the index's scale.

Place with the worst climate

Based on the Climate Severity Index, the nation's worst climate was in a place that no longer exists. The weather station at Isachsen, Northwest Territories, which was closed in 1978, registered 99 out of 100 on the index's scale.

First billion-dollar disaster

The storm's moniker has a nice ring to it, but there was nothing nice about the disaster. The first billion-dollar disaster in Canadian history was the flood that hit Saguenay, Quebec, from July 18 to 21, 1996. Roads and bridges throughout the area were destroyed, 12,000 residents were evacuated and 10 people were killed.

Deadliest sinkhole

The deadliest recorded sinkhole in Canada happened on May 4, 1971, when heavy rain created a sinkhole 600 m wide and 30 m deep in St-Jean-Vianney, Quebec. The hole and associated mudslide claimed the lives of 31 people and swallowed 35 homes, a bus and several cars.

Worst rig disaster

The worst disaster involving an offshore drilling rig in Canada (and the third-worst in the world) was the sinking of the Ocean Ranger on February 15, 1982. At the time, it was the largest semi-submersible drilling rig in existence. The Ocean Ranger sank 300 km off the coast of Newfoundland in winds of 145 km per hour and waves 21 m high. Eighty-four people were killed.

Biggest wave

This is one seriously big wave! On September 11, 1995, the QE2 ocean liner was caught in Hurricane Luis off the coast of Newfoundland and was hit by a 30 m wave. This is the largest wave height ever recorded. The storm was also gigantic: it covered almost the entire north Atlantic.

Invention of the UV index

For a nation that's undoubtedly well known for its cool climate, it seems somewhat surprising that Canadians invented the UV Index, a measure of the intensity of the sun's ultraviolet radiation in the sunburn spectrum. As UV increases, the sun's rays can do more damage to skin, eyes and the immune system. In 1992, scientists at Environment Canada developed the index as a health protection tool for Canadians, and it is now forecast for 48 locations across the country.

The Independence hurricane

A horrid hurricane. The Newfoundland Hurricane of 1775 was probably part of the same storm that was dubbed the "Independence Hurricane" in the United States. It was by far the most deadly to have occurred in what is present-day Canada. The storm killed more than 4,000 mariners, destroying the entire Newfoundland fishing fleet as well as some British warships. It also killed hundreds and wrecked havoc along the eastern seaboard of present-day United States. It came at a crucial point at the beginning of the American War of Independence — hence its name.

Longest mammal migration

The humpback whale makes the longest migration of any mammal on the planet. The species travels up to 8,500 km one way. The north Pacific population that travels through Canadian waters journeys from Alaska to the tropical seas off Hawaii.

Largest beaver dam

DAM! The world's largest beaver dam (spotted on satellite images by the scientists who discovered it) is also found in Wood Buffalo National Park.

Biggest land animal

The largest land animal in North America is the wood bison, which can be found in Alberta, Manitoba and the Northwest Territories. Mature males can reach 3.8 m in length, stand 2 m high at the shoulder and can weigh up to 900 kg. It's believed there were once more than 168,000 wood bison in Canada, but hunting and severe winters have decimated the population. Today the country is home to only about 10,000 of these animals.

LARGEST HERD OF WOOD BISON

When it comes to world wildlife records, Wood Buffalo National Park, which straddles the Alberta/Northwest Territories border, claims quite a few. For starters, it's home to the world's largest herd of wood bison.

Biggest animal

The biggest animal on Earth calls Canada home (at least part of the time). Blue whales, which can grow up to 27 m long and weigh up to 132 tonnes, are found in Canadian waters along Canada's east coast. Not only are blue whales the largest creature on the planet, they're also the loudest. Their cry can reach 186 decibels, louder than a jet plane.

Biggest fish

The largest fish swimming in Canadian waters is the basking shark, which can grow to more than 6 m long and weigh up to 4,500 kg. It's also the second-largest shark and fish in the world. Basking sharks are often seen in Canadian waters in the summer and fall near coastal areas of Atlantic Canada.

Fastest animal

The pronghorn antelope, found in southern Alberta and Saskatchewan, is the fastest land animal in North America, capable of reaching speeds up to 72 km per hour in short bursts and sustaining speeds up to 60 km per hour over longer distances. Its speeds over longer distance lead some to consider it the fastest land animal in the world.

ONLY NESTING WHOOPING CRANES

Wood Buffalo National Park is home to the world's only nesting site of the endangered whooping cranes.

Fastest bird

You do NOT want to be the prey of the peregrine falcon. Why? When hunting, peregrines can dive at more than 300 km per hour, making them the fastest bird in the world. The highest recorded speed of a peregrine is reported to be 389 km per hour. Here's hoping the prey don't even see it coming.

Longest bird migration

Too bad there are no frequent flyer miles for birds. If there were, the Arctic tern would earn lots of free flights. After all, the small seabird, which summers in Canada's north, has the longest migration of any bird in the world. It travels some 40,000 km from its Arctic breeding grounds to its winter home near Antarctica and back again.

Longest butterfly migration

It weighs about as much as a paper clip, but the monarch butterfly doesn't let its small size get in the way of travelling great distances. The monarch butterfly makes the longest migration of all insect species. Experts believe that monarchs travel at least 4,600 km, but it's possible that they fly twice as far as that. Individuals migrate from southern Canada to wintering areas in Mexico each fall.

Largest goose colony

By the sound of all the honking, you'd think it was one serious traffic jam. But no, it's just the world's largest goose colony, home to an estimated 1.7 million lesser snow geese. The federal Dewey Soper Migratory Bird Sanctuary on Nunavut's Baffin Island has an estimated one third of all lesser snows on the planet, along with significant populations of other birds.

First waterfowl refuge

Saskatchewan's Last Mountain Lake Bird Sanctuary was the first waterfowl refuge in North America. It was established in 1887. More than 280 species of birds have been recorded in the 15,600-hectare sanctuary, and more than 100 of these species breed there. It's also an important area for migratory birds, and in the fall up to 50,000 sandhill cranes, 450,000 geese and several hundred thousand ducks pass through — often in flocks of tens of thousands.

Largest puffin colony

The largest colony of Atlantic puffins in North America is found in Newfoundland's Witless Bay Ecological Reserve. The reserve, made up of four islands — Gull, Green, Great and Pee Pee — sees more than 260,000 pairs of puffins nest there in late spring and summer. The puffin is Newfoundland and Labrador's official bird.

First migratory waterfowl refuge

Jack Miner, known as the "Father of Conservation," is considered the founder of the migratory waterfowl refuge system. He founded the first such reserve, the Jack Miner Migratory Bird Sanctuary, in 1904 in Kingsville, Ontario.

Largest bird sanctuary

If birds have a heaven on Earth, it must be the Queen Maud Gulf Migratory Bird Sanctuary on the Arctic Ocean coast in Nunavut. It's the country's largest migratory bird sanctuary and Canada's largest federally protected area, measuring some 61,765 square km. There are about 60 goose colonies in the area. One contains 90 percent of the world population of Ross' Geese and another has more than 30 percent of the Western Canadian Arctic population of lesser snow geese.

LARGEST STORM-PETREL COLONY

The Witless Bay Ecological Reserve (see Largest puffin colony, left) is also home to the continent's largest colony of Leach's storm-petrel, a small black seabird. The second largest such colony in the world, it is home to more than 620,000 pairs that nest on the island each year.

First banded birds

Five years after Jack Miner (see previous) established the world's first migratory bird reserve, he created the concept of banding birds to trace the migratory periods and routes of waterfowl. Ever since, the practice has been instrumental in the protection of migratory birds in North America and the world.

Most polar bears

Canada has two-thirds of the Earth's population of polar bears, the world's largest terrestrial carnivore. Adult males average between 400 and 600 kg, with some exceeding 800 kg. Polar bears are also the largest species of bears.

Longest snake

No matter what you call it, this is one long snake. And the longest native snake you'll find in Canada. Once known as the black ratsnake, but today called the gray ratsnake, the species is known to grow to 1.5 m and even longer. It is an excellent climber and is sometimes found in the cavities of hollow trees. It is typically found in southwestern Ontario north of Lake Erie and in the Rideau Lakes area from Kingston to Smith Falls.

Freshwater harbor seals

In the Nunavik region of Quebec, about 250 km east of Hudson Bay, lies a very unique population of harbour seals — the planet's only population of the species that lives year round in fresh water. Known as the Lac des Loups Marins harbour seals, experts believe the animals were separated from their original marine habitat 3,000 to 8,000 years ago. It's estimated that there are 50 to 600 of the seals, which are considered endangered.

Most snakes

If you've got ophidiophobia (a fear of snakes), DON'T stop here. Manitoba's Narcisse Wildlife Management Area has the largest concentration of snakes in the world. It's estimated that up to 70,000 snakes use hibernacula (hibernation sites) here, particularly the red-sided garter snake. The snakes emerge in massive wriggly masses on the first warm days of May. In fact, Mother's Day, of all days, is often a prime time to see the spectacle.

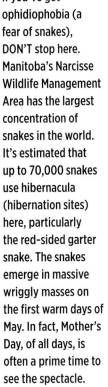

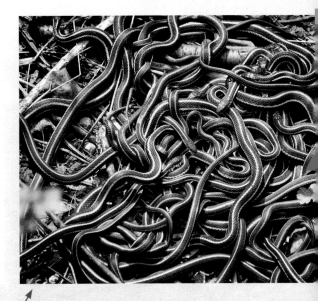

First protected area for grizzly bears

British Columbia's Khutzeymateen Provincial Park was the first area in the country specifically protected for grizzly bears. Established in 1994, and also known as the Khutzeymateen/K'tsim-a-deen Grizzly Sanctuary, or "Valley of the Grizzly," the 43,000- hectare park is located 45 km northeast of Prince Rupert and is home to about 50 grizzlies — one of the largest populations of the species in the province.

Smallest bird

Keep your eyes peeled: Canada's smallest bird is the calliope hummingbird, which is about 7 cm long (shown life size here) and weighs just 2.5 g. It's found in central British Columbia and southwestern Alberta.

Largest rodent

Know what Canada's largest rodent is? We're so proud of it we put it on our nickel, and it's celebrated as a symbol of Canadiana. Yes, the beaver — which attained official status as a national emblem on March 24, 1975.

Biggest moose

If there's a critter synonymous with Canada's hinterland, it's undoubtedly the moose. Not only is the moose the largest member of the deer family, but the *Alces alces giga* subspecies (giant moose), found in western Yukon, is the largest of the species. Adult males measure up to 2.1 m tall at the shoulder, are about 2.7 m long and can weigh up to 725 kg. Indeed, on September 25, 2013, hunter Heinz Naef from Dawson City took a moose weighing in at more than 560 kg, which is now a new world record.

Smallest mammal

They weigh just 12.4 g, so it's little wonder that the pygmy shrew is the smallest mammal in the Americas. Looking like something between a mouse and a mole, shrews are small: the pygmy's head and body average length is about 5.1 to 6.4 cm. They can be found throughout most of eastern Canada.

Biggest waterfowl

Cue the horns. The trumpeter swan is the largest species of native waterfowl in North America. Males weigh an average 12 kg, while females are slightly smaller, averaging 10 kg. In Canada, trumpeters are found in British Columbia, the Northwest Territories and the Yukon.

World's deadliest creature

Believe it or not, what many consider the world's deadliest creature lives right here in Canada. And they're found virtually everywhere. Fortunately for Canadians, the mosquito's bite here is largely just itchy. Around the world, however, mosquitoes carry and pass along malaria-causing parasites. The World Heath Organization estimates that in 2010 malaria killed between 537,000 and 907,000 people, mostly children under five years old in Africa.

Birds' deadliest enemies

Sorry cat lovers, but your cuddly kittens are actually brutal killers. According to a 2013 study by Environment Canada, predation by cats is the largest human-related cause of death for birds in Canada. Urban pet cats are estimated to be responsible for about one-sixth of all bird deaths in the country, while feral cats (just 25 percent of all cats) are responsible for 59 percent of bird deaths. Outdoor cats are estimated to be responsible for the deaths of between 105 and 348 million birds per year.

Largest maple leaf

Here's a record with a special Canadian connection. The largest recorded maple leaf (actual leaf!) was found on December 14, 2010, in Richmond, British Columbia, by Vikas Tanwar and family. The leaf — 53 cm wide, 52.2 cm tall, with a 32.5 cm stem — was confirmed as the biggest ever found by Guinness World Records.

Tallest tree

You could call it the green giant. Canada's tallest recorded tree stands 56 m high. The western red cedar, located in British Columbia's Pacific Rim National Park, was discovered in 1988 and has been nicknamed "Cheewhat Giant" because of its proximity to Cheewhat Lake. The diameter of the tree is more than 6 m and contains an estimated 450 cubic m in timber volume.

Oldest maple tree

Canada's known for many things, and a big one is maple syrup. The oldest known sugar maple tree in the country is estimated to be at least 500 years old, and it's found in southwestern Ontario's North Pelham area. The Comfort Maple, as it's known, stands about 30.5 m tall and has a trunk circumference of 6 m.

Largest indoor aquarium

Ripley's Aquarium of Canada in Toronto is the nation's largest indoor aquarium. The 12,500 square m attraction, which opened on October 16, 2013, boasts more than 16,000 marine animals and more than 450 species.

First aquarium

Vancouver Aquarium, located in the city's Stanley Park, was the country's first. When it opened on June 15, 1956, the aquarium was a 830 square m facility. Today, it's more than 9,000 square m.

First orca study

The Vancouver Aquarium (see First aquarium) was the first facility in the world to study an orca. The aquarium acquired killer whale Moby Doll, a young male, in July 1969.

Most sharks

Ripley's Aquarium of Canada (see above) is home to the largest collection of sharks in North America. One of the facility's highlights is the Shark Lagoon, which features a 96 m tunnel walkway through a 2.84-million-litre tank, where you can see sand tiger sharks that measure 3 to 3.7 m.

Oldest reptiles

The fossils of the reptiles whose descendents would become dinosaurs and mammals can be found at the Joggins Fossil Cliffs in Nova Scotia. These 315-million-year-old fossils are the world's oldest known reptiles. They come from a time when giant seed fern trees, insects, primitive lobe-finned fish and amphibians roamed the Earth. The fossils are visible simply from a walk on Joggins beach.

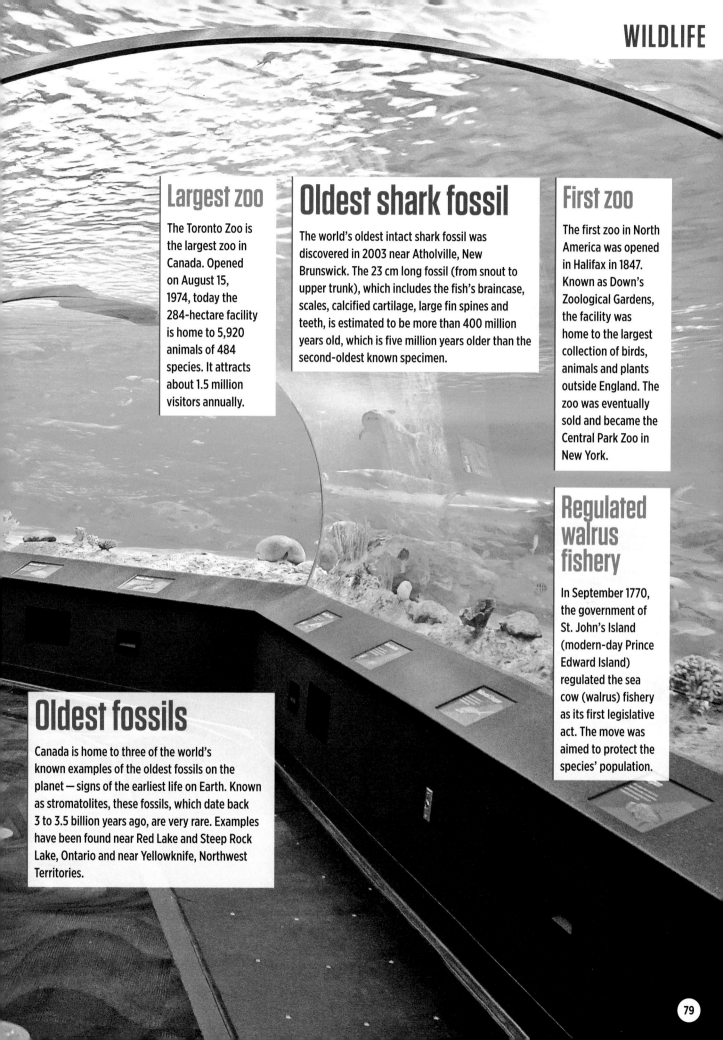

Largest zoo

The Toronto Zoo is the largest zoo in Canada. Opened on August 15, 1974, today the 284-hectare facility is home to 5,920 animals of 484 species. It attracts about 1.5 million visitors annually.

Oldest shark fossil

The world's oldest intact shark fossil was discovered in 2003 near Atholville, New Brunswick. The 23 cm long fossil (from snout to upper trunk), which includes the fish's braincase, scales, calcified cartilage, large fin spines and teeth, is estimated to be more than 400 million years old, which is five million years older than the second-oldest known specimen.

First zoo

The first zoo in North America was opened in Halifax in 1847. Known as Down's Zoological Gardens, the facility was home to the largest collection of birds, animals and plants outside England. The zoo was eventually sold and became the Central Park Zoo in New York.

Regulated walrus fishery

In September 1770, the government of St. John's Island (modern-day Prince Edward Island) regulated the sea cow (walrus) fishery as its first legislative act. The move was aimed to protect the species' population.

Oldest fossils

Canada is home to three of the world's known examples of the oldest fossils on the planet — signs of the earliest life on Earth. Known as stromatolites, these fossils, which date back 3 to 3.5 billion years ago, are very rare. Examples have been found near Red Lake and Steep Rock Lake, Ontario and near Yellowknife, Northwest Territories.

Biggest lake trout (1)

If there's a freshwater fish synonymous with Canada, it's got to be the lake trout. It should come as no surprise that the largest laker ever recorded was caught by a commercial angler in Saskatchewan's Lake Athabasca in 1961. The trout measured 126 cm long and weighed 43.6 kg.

Biggest lake trout (2)

The sport angling world-record lake trout also came from Canadian waters: a 32.7 kg fish caught in Great Bear Lake, Northwest Territories in 1995.

Biggest brook trout

If you're an angler in Canada, you're undoubtedly familiar with the legendary Cook brook trout. Caught in July 1916 by Dr. J.W. Cook in Ontario's Nipigon River, the 6.6 kg brookie has stood as the world record for the species for nearly a century. In fact, it's one of the longest-standing angling records on Earth.

Largest and oldest freshwater fish

The white sturgeon is the largest and longest-living freshwater fish in North America. In Canada, the species can be found in a number of rivers in British Columbia, including the Fraser, Kootenay, Nechako and Columbia. Specimens more than 6 m in length and estimated to be more than 100 years old have been recorded in the Fraser River.

BIGGEST ARCTIC CHAR

The International Game Fish Association all-tackle world record for Arctic char was caught in the Northwest Territories' Tree River on July 31, 1981. The char weighed 14.77 kg.

BIGGEST LAKE STURGEON

Another big fish story. The International Game Fish Association all-tackle world-record lake sturgeon was caught in Ontario's Georgian Bay on May 29, 1982. The behemoth weighed a whopping 76.2 kg.

Biggest Arctic grayling

Perhaps it should come as little surprise, given our expanse of Arctic, that the International Game Fishing Association all-tackle world record for Arctic grayling was caught in Canada. The record grayling was nabbed on August 16, 1967 in the Katseyedie River, Northwest Territories, and tipped the scales at 2.69 kg.

Biggest salmon

With Canada's world-renowned salmon runs, is it any wonder the country holds a salmon angling world record? The International Game Fish Association all-tackle world record for chum salmon, a 15.87 kg fish, was caught on July 11, 1995, in Edye Pass, British Columbia.

Biggest splake

Given that it's somewhat of a uniquely Canadian species, it's hardly surprising that the International Game Fish Association all-tackle world record for splake was caught here. The 9.39 kg fish was hauled from Ontario's Georgian Bay on May 17, 1987.

Unique brook trout

The Aurora trout, a unique strain of brook trout, is found only in Ontario and Quebec. The original strain of the fish was extirpated from its original native lakes in Ontario's Temagami region. Captive breeding led to the reintroduction of the species to a select group of lakes in the 1990s.

Biggest Aurora trout

It kind of figures that the International Game Fish Association all-tackle world record for Aurora trout comes from Canada. The 2.21 kg fish was caught in Ontario's Carol Lake on October 8, 1996.

BIGGEST LAKE WHITEFISH

The International Game Fish Association all-tackle world record lake whitefish was caught on May 21, 1984, in Meaford, Ontario. The fish weighed 6.52 kg.

Biggest rainbow trout

What's at the end of a rainbow? Who cares, when it's a world-record rainbow trout. The International Game Fish Association all-tackle world-record rainbow, a 21.77 kg specimen, was caught on September 5, 2009, in Saskatchewan's Lake Diefenbaker.

Biggest rock bass

What a big red eye you have! One of the two fish tied for the International Game Fish Association all-tackle world-record rock bass — a species recognizable by its distinctive red eye — was caught in Ontario's York River on August 1, 1974. The rock weighed 1.36 kg.

Original Canadian fish

Take a male brook trout and cross it with a female lake trout and what do you get? Arguably a uniquely Canadian fish, the splake. While previous records exist of the hybrid, it wasn't until after experiments made in 1947 by J.E. Stenton, a warden at Alberta's Banff National Park, that the first official crosses of the species were made by the Quebec Department of Fish and Game in 1948.

BIGGEST STONE SHEEP

More really big horns. The world-record Stone's sheep, according to the Boone and Crocket Club, was taken in 1936 by L.S. Chadwick near Muskwa River, British Columbia. The sheep scored 196⅝.

Biggest bighorn sheep

This bighorn sheep really did have big horns. The world record bighorn sheep was taken near Luscar Mountain, Alberta, by Guinn D. Crousen in 2000. The Boone and Crockett Club, the international keeper of such records, scored the animal 208⅜. The score is based on a combination of characteristics of the horns.

Biggest whitetail deer

With a name like Biggar, is it any wonder that the Saskatchewan town has the world record for the largest typical whitetail deer taken by a hunter? The Boone and Crockett Club scored the deer 213⅝.The score is based on a combination of the length of the antlers and the number of points they have. The big buck was taken by hunter Milo Hanson in November 1993.

Biggest Canada moose

This was one big moose. According to the Boone & Crockett Club, the world-record Canada species moose was taken in 1980 by Michael E. Laub near British Columbia's Grayling River. The moose scored 242.

Biggest cougar

Here's one colossal cat: according to the Boone and Crockett Club, the world-record cougar was taken in 1979 by Douglas E. Schuk near Tatlayoko Lake, British Columbia. It scored 16⁴⁄₁₆ (the score is based on the skull's width and length).

Biggest mule deer

According to the Boone and Crockett Club, the world-record non-typical mule deer was taken near Chip Lake, Alberta, by Ed Broder in 1926. (Non-typical refers to abnormal antler growth.) The deer received a score of 355⅔.

BIGGEST SITKA BLACKTAIL DEER

The world-record Sitka blacktail deer, according to the Boone and Crockett Club was taken in 1970 by Peter Bond near Juskatla, British Columbia. The deer scored 133.

Biggest mountain caribou

Canada is renowned for its caribou populations, and it's home to some of the largest antlered caribou ever recorded. The world-record mountain caribou, according to the Boone and Crockett Club, was taken in the Yukon's Pelly Mountains in 1988 by Paul T. Deuling. It scored 459⅜.

Biggest Central Canada barren-ground caribou

Another big 'bou: according to the Boone and Crockett Club, the world-record, Central Canada barren-ground caribou, which scored 433⅘, was taken by Donald J. Hotter III in 1994 near Humpy Lake, Northwest Territories.

Biggest Quebec-Labrador caribou

And yet another world-best 'bou: the world-record Quebec-Labrador caribou was taken near Nain, Labrador, by Zack Elbox in 1931, and scored 474⅝, according to the Boone & Crockett Club.

Biggest woodland caribou

And another — in 1910, an unknown hunter in Newfoundland took the world-record woodland caribou. It scored 419⅝, according to the Boone and Crockett Club.

Scraping the sky

Canada's tallest buildings

	Name	Location	Storeys/Height		Year Opened
1.	First Canadian Place	Toronto	72	298 m	1975
2.	Scotia Plaza	Toronto	68	275 m	1988
3.	Aura	Toronto	78	273 m	2014
4.	Canada Trust Tower	Toronto	53	261 m	1990
5.	Trump International Hotel & Tower Toronto	Toronto	57	257 m	2012
6.	Commerce Court West	Toronto	57	239 m	1972
7.	The Bow	Calgary	58	236 m	2012
8.	Le 1250 Boulevard René-Lévesque	Montréal	47	226 m	1992
9.	TD Tower	Toronto	56	223 m	1967
10.	Bay Adelaide West	Toronto	51	218 m	2009

First retractable roof

Toronto's Rogers Centre boasted the world's first fully retractable roof when the building opened in June 1989 (at the time it was called SkyDome). The 11,000-tonne roof is made of four sections and opens (and closes) in a semi-circular motion in 20 minutes. The current home of Major League Baseball's Toronto Blue Jays and the Canadian Football League's Toronto Argonauts, the stadium also hosts numerous other sporting and entertainment events. Indeed, more than 60 million people have passed through the building's turnstiles.

Tallest tower

It's since been eclipsed, but for 34 years (1976–2010) Toronto's CN Tower put the country on the world map as home to the globe's tallest tower, building and freestanding structure. Though it now ranks third tallest, at a mere 553.33 m, it's still no less impressive. Approximately 1.5 million people visit the tower each year, for attractions that include a lookout, a glass floor, a revolving restaurant and the EdgeWalk (the world's highest, hands-free walk on a 1.5 m ledge encircling the building, 365 m up).

Tallest building

At 72 storeys and 298 m high, Toronto's First Canadian Place is the country's tallest building (not tower, please note). The 2.6 million square m skyscraper was considered ahead of its time when it opened in 1975, and extensive interior and exterior rejuvenation was completed in October 2012. With the highest rooftop in Canada, it also serves as a prime communications site, second only to the nearby CN Tower.

Tiny house

It's hard to say what record, if any, the tiny house at 128 Day Avenue in Toronto holds, but there's no doubt it's one small house. Measuring 2.2 m wide and 14.3 m long, the home was built in 1912. It's still lived in today and has its own website, thelittlehouse.ca.

Largest stadium

Montreal's Olympic Stadium is the country's largest stadium based on seating capacity. Opened in 1976 for the Summer Olympics, the 56,000-seat stadium has seen more than 67 million visitors since it opened.

Largest sports complex

Whitby, Ontario, located about an hour east of Toronto, is the home of the country's largest municipally owned and operated multi-use sports complex. The Iroquois Park Sports Centre houses six arenas, a 25 m deep swimming pool, six tennis courts, four baseball diamonds, one lit soccer field, and a strength and conditioning training centre. It is surrounded by 20 hectares of parkland.

Biggest church

Saint Joseph's Oratory of Mount Royal is Canada's largest church. The Roman Catholic minor basilica on Westmount Summit in Montreal opened in 1967 and can seat 10,000. More than two million visitors and pilgrims visit the church each year. The building's granite exterior was constructed with blocks cut from Lac Mégantic quarries.

Largest hockey arena

The largest hockey arena in Canada? Montreal's Bell Centre, home of the Montreal Canadiens, which has a capacity of 21,273 seats. The arena, known as the Molson Centre when it opened in 1996, is considered one of the most technologically advanced and versatile entertainment facilities in the world. More than one million hockey fans visit the building annually and 650,000 more people attend the arena for other events.

Oldest wooden house

There's a special house at 477 St. George Street in Annapolis Royal, Nova Scotia. The privately owned house, a provincially and municipally designated heritage building, is the oldest wooden house in Canada. The original house was built in 1693, but was burned in 1707, only to be rebuilt in 1708 on the original foundation.

BIGGEST CEMETERY

Montreal's Notre-Dame-des-Neiges Cemetery is the largest in Canada and the third-largest on the continent. The Catholic cemetery was founded in 1854 and has more than 65,000 monuments and 71 family vaults. More than 175,000 people visit the cemetery annually.

Biggest mosque

Baitunnur Mosque in Calgary is the largest Muslim mosque complex in the country at 4,460 square m.

Biggest seats

Those seats at your local stadium feeling small? Time to visit Hamilton's Tim Hortons Field, the home of the Canadian Football League's Hamilton Tiger-Cats, which opened in 2014. The stadium's luxuries include the largest individual seats of any outdoor sports building in Canada (53 to 61 cm wide, depending their location in the facility) and more leg room than any other comparable stadium.

First planetarium

Sit back and enjoy the view. Canada's first planetarium, the Queen Elizabeth II Planetarium in Edmonton, opened on September 22, 1960. The planetarium closed on December 31, 1983.

First movie theatre

Pass the popcorn. The first commercial movie theatre in North America opened on January 1, 1906, in Montreal. The Ouimetoscope was converted from a tavern to a 500-seat cinema with a small screen.

First two-screen cinema

Ottawa's Elgin Street Theatre was the first in the world to have two screens, allowing customers to choose between watching one of two movies in one venue. The second screen was added in 1957 by owner Nathan Taylor, who would go on to create the Cineplex Odeon chain.

First Canadian mosque

The Baitul-Islam Mosque in Vaughan, Ontario, just north of Toronto, was the first Muslim mosque in Canada. It opened on October 17, 1992.

First drive-in

The nation's first drive-in theatre opened in Stoney Creek, Ontario, in 1946. The Skyway had a 750-car capacity.

First milk pasteurization

The Hospital for Sick Children installed the first milk pasteurization plant in Canada in 1908 — 30 years before the process was mandatory.

First opera and ballet theatre

One of a kind: the Four Seasons Centre for the Performing Arts in Toronto was the first theatre in Canada built specifically for opera and ballet performances. Opened in 2006, the facility features a modern take on the traditional horseshoe-shaped auditorium, which delivers great sightlines and acoustics. The building is the permanent home of the Canadian Opera Company.

First hospital

Quebec City's Hôtel-Dieu was the first hospital in America north of Mexico. It was founded by three Augustinian nuns in 1639.

First public hospital

John Molson, founder of the brewing company, was instrumental in the establishment of Montreal's first public hospital, Montreal General Hospital. It opened on May 1, 1819.

Largest children's hospital

If buildings had a heart, this one's would be pretty big. Toronto's Hospital for Sick Children, known as SickKids, is the country' largest facility dedicated to children's health. The hospital's history dates back to 1875, and today about 15,000 youngsters stay at the facility each year, while another nearly 300,000 visit the hospital's more than 100 clinics annually.

Benjamin Franklin and Canadian mail

Do you know the important Canadian connection to Benjamin Franklin? In 1753, he was named joint deputy postmaster-general for the British colonies and opened the first post office in Canada in Halifax.

First theatre

More Molson. John Molson also helped build Montreal's first permanent theatre. Molson was a major shareholder of the company that built Theatre Royal, which opened in 1825. The 1,000-seat facility ran 111 full-length plays in one season before the company went bankrupt in 1826.

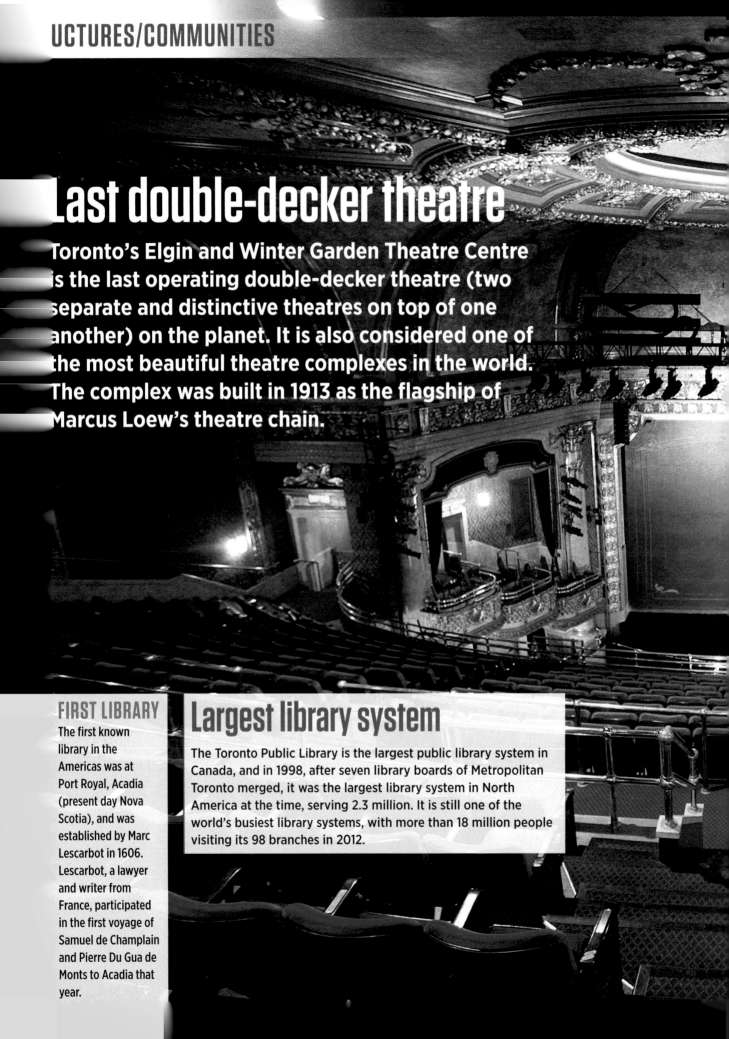

Last double-decker theatre

Toronto's Elgin and Winter Garden Theatre Centre is the last operating double-decker theatre (two separate and distinctive theatres on top of one another) on the planet. It is also considered one of the most beautiful theatre complexes in the world. The complex was built in 1913 as the flagship of Marcus Loew's theatre chain.

FIRST LIBRARY

The first known library in the Americas was at Port Royal, Acadia (present day Nova Scotia), and was established by Marc Lescarbot in 1606. Lescarbot, a lawyer and writer from France, participated in the first voyage of Samuel de Champlain and Pierre Du Gua de Monts to Acadia that year.

Largest library system

The Toronto Public Library is the largest public library system in Canada, and in 1998, after seven library boards of Metropolitan Toronto merged, it was the largest library system in North America at the time, serving 2.3 million. It is still one of the world's busiest library systems, with more than 18 million people visiting its 98 branches in 2012.

Largest capitol building

The prairie vistas are not the only big things in Saskatchewan. The province's Legislative Building in Regina is the largest capitol building in Canada. Planning for the building began less than a year after Saskatchewan became a province on September 1, 1905. The home of Saskatchewan's Legislative Assembly, the building opened on October 12, 1912, and is surrounded by one of the largest urban parks in North America. The façade and interior reflect the beaux-arts architectural style of the time.

Oldest courthouse

There's been a lot of order in this court. The Argyle Township Court House & Gaol, in Tusket, Nova Scotia, is the country's oldest standing courthouse. Built in 1805, it was a court and jail from its opening until 1944.

Biggest jail

Go to jail, go directly to Canada's biggest jail — the Edmonton Remand Centre. The facility has space for 1,952 beds and is the size of 10 CFL football fields: 59,511 square m.

Smallest jail

Hope you're not a claustrophobic crook. The Rodney Jail, in Rodney, Ontario, bills itself as the smallest jail in North America. Built in 1890, the jail is 4.57 by 5.49 m.

Largest military training area

Canadian Forces Base Suffield, north of Medicine Hat, Alberta, is the nation's largest military training area in Canada. The base, which falls under the command of the 3rd Canadian Division, covers 2,690 square km.

Biggest shopping mall

Edmonton is home to the largest mall in North America, the West Edmonton Mall, at 4.9 million square m. From 1981 until 2004 it was the largest mall in the world. The shopping centre boasts 800 stores and services, including 2 hotels and more than 100 restaurants. Approximately 30.8 million shoppers descend on it each year. That's serious retail therapy.

Biggest indoor amusement park

The West Edmonton Mall's Galaxyland is the world's largest indoor amusement park. It features 24 rides and attractions.

Biggest indoor triple-loop roller coaster

West Edmonton Mall boasts the world's largest indoor triple-loop roller coaster, the Mindbender, which is part of the mall's Galaxyland amusement park.

Biggest parking lot

Looking for a parking spot? At West Edmonton Mall, that shouldn't be a problem. The mall boasts the planet's largest parking lot, with a capacity for 20,000 vehicles. A lot adjacent to the mall has space for another 10,000 cars.

Biggest indoor miniature golf course

West Edmonton Mall is also home to the world's largest indoor miniature golf course. Professor WEM's Adventure Golf Course features 18 holes, complete with sand traps and water hazards.

BIGGEST INDOOR LAKE

West Edmonton Mall is home to the world's largest permanent indoor lake. The lake includes an exact replica of the Santa Maria, the flagship of Christopher Columbus' 1492 expedition to North America.

BIGGEST INDOOR WAVE POOL

West Edmonton Mall is also home to the globe's largest indoor wave pool, which is part of the mall's World Waterpark.

Biggest snow playground

Like to play in the snow? Check out the largest snow playground in North America, which is created annually each winter for Winterlude, held in Ottawa and Gatineau, Quebec. The Snowflake Kingdom, as the playground is known, is built in Gatineau's Jacques Cartier Park and features gigantic snow slides, a winter obstacle course, a giant maze and much more.

Biggest water park

The Calypso water park near Ottawa is the nation's largest. The 40-hectare park, which opened on June 7, 2010, features 100 different water attractions to keep visitors cool.

FIRST SHOPPING MALL

Attention shoppers: Park Royal Shopping Centre in Vancouver is considered Canada's first shopping mall. It opened in September 1950.

Most roller coasters

Looking for a roller coaster? Canada's Wonderland, north of Toronto, is home to the continent's largest variety of roller coasters, with 16. The park's longest and faster coaster is the Leviathan, which measures 1,672 m and reaches a top speed of 148 km per hour.

Biggest amusement park

The name is bang-on. Canada's Wonderland, located in Vaughan, Ontario, just north of Toronto, is the nation's largest amusement park and one of the largest in North America. Opened on May 23, 1981, the park features more than 200 attractions, 69 rides, an eight-hectare water park and live shows.

One-of-a-kind thrill ride

Looking for a unique thrill? The Sledge Hammer ride at Canada's Wonderland is one of a kind. The attraction, which debuted in 2003, lifts riders 24.3 m in the air in 4- to 8-person gondolas, then takes them through a series of jumps and freefalls that lasts 1 minute and 43 seconds, reaching a top speed of 65 km per hour.

First WindSeeker swing ride

Canada's Wonderland's WindSeeker swing ride, which ascends 91.75 m and swings riders at a 45-degree angle at speeds of up to 50 km per hour, was the first such ride in the world. The ride lasts three minutes.

Biggest outdoor wave pool

White Water Bay at the Splash Works water park in Canada's Wonderland is the largest outdoor wave pool in the nation. It would take 90 gallons of paint to paint the bottom of the pool.

Longest cantilever bridge

The Quebec Bridge in Quebec City, which crosses the St. Lawrence River, is the longest span cantilever bridge in Canada, and at the time of its completion in 1917 it was the largest in the world. It is also the longest cantilever railroad span ever. The single span stretches nearly 550 m. The bridge's construction is also famed, as it took three attempts and cost 89 lives before it was finally completed.

Longest and highest trestle bridge

The High Level Bridge in Lethbridge, Alberta, is the world's longest and highest trestle bridge. There are higher and longer trestle bridges, but none match the combination of length and height of the High Level.) The bridge, which opened November 1, 1909, spans 1,623 m and runs 95.7 m above the Oldman River.

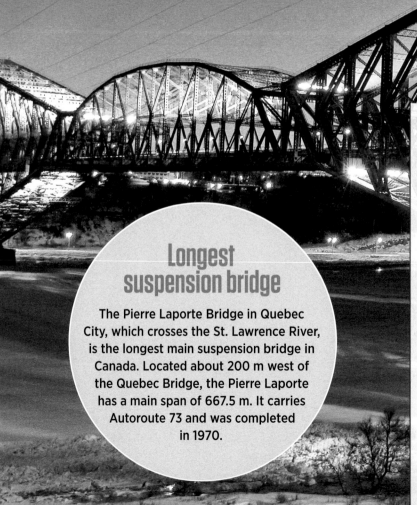

Longest bridge over icy waters

Opened on May 31, 1997, at a cost of $1 billion, the Confederation Bridge (linking Prince Edward Island and New Brunswick) is the largest bridge in the world that crosses ice-covered waters. Prince Edward Islanders voted to replace the ferry service connecting the island to the mainland with the curved, 12.9 km bridge. In a plebiscite in 1988, 59.4 percent of voters preferred the fixed link.

Longest suspension bridge

The Pierre Laporte Bridge in Quebec City, which crosses the St. Lawrence River, is the longest main suspension bridge in Canada. Located about 200 m west of the Quebec Bridge, the Pierre Laporte has a main span of 667.5 m. It carries Autoroute 73 and was completed in 1970.

Busiest bridge

The Champlain Bridge, which crosses the St. Lawrence River in Montreal, is the busiest crossing in Canada. It's estimated that about 50 to 60 million vehicles, 6.2 million trucks, 200,000 buses and 11 million transit users cross the bridge each year. About $20 billion in international trade travels the Champlain annually, and it is vital to regional and national economies.

Longest historical suspension bridge

Looking for a swinging good time? Try the Souris Swinging Bridge in Souris, Manitoba, the nation's longest historical suspension bridge. Open to pedestrian traffic, the 177.4 m bridge was originally built in 1904. The bridge was lost in 1976 when it was taken out by water and ice, but was rebuilt and has been commemorated on a Canada Post stamp.

LONGEST BRIDGE

When it officially opened on August 25, 1860, Montreal's Victoria Bridge was the longest bridge in the world. Built as a railway bridge crossing the St. Lawrence River and connecting Montreal and Saint-Lambert, Quebec, the bridge was considered a modern world wonder at the time of its construction. It was the first structure to cross the St. Lawrence.

Tallest timber trestle bridge

The Kinsol Trestle near the village of Shawnigan on Vancouver Island is the country's tallest timber trestle. It is also one of the largest timber bridges in the world and the highest timber trestle remaining in the Commonwealth. The 44 m high, 188 m long bridge crosses the Koksilah River. It was built in 1920.

Longest pedestrian bridge

Originally built as a railway bridge, the 914 m viaduct in Outlook, Saskatchewan, is the country's longest pedestrian bridge. Crossing the South Saskatchewan River and part of the Trans Canada Trail, the bridge operated as a railway bridge from October 23, 1912 until March 16, 1987.

Longest covered bridge

The longest covered bridge on Earth is the Hartland Covered Bridge in Hartland, New Brunswick. The 391 m bridge was built in 1897 and was covered in 1921–22. Its covering was controversial, as covered bridges were known as "kissing bridges" — horse and wagon traffic would stop half way across so that riders could lock lips. Some locals feared covering the bridge would destroy the morals of their young people.

Oldest incorporated city

The oldest incorporated city in Canada? None other than Saint John, New Brunswick. At the end of the 1776 American Revolution, 14,000 American supporters of the British established two settlements at the mouth of the Saint John River (one on each side; Parrtown on the east and Carleton on the west). In 1785, the two settlements merged to form Canada's first city. Saint John is also the only city on the world-famous Bay of Fundy.

Oldest city

St. John's, Newfoundland, is the most easterly city in North America. But it also claims to be the continent's oldest city. St. John's has long been a centre of fisheries in the New World — the earliest records of battles over control of the city's port date back to 1555.

First English colony

There are some great place names in Newfoundland and Labrador (Come By Chance and Heart's Content, for instance). Cupids is another. But the town on Conception Bay is significant for more than just its unique name. It was the first English colony in Canada and also the oldest continuously occupied English settlement in the country. In 1610, English colonist John Guy established a plantation at was then known as Cuper's Cove.

Oldest French community

Tadoussac, Quebec, is well known as a launching point for great whale watching in the St. Lawrence River. It's also the oldest continuously inhabited French community in America. Known as the cradle of New France, Tadoussac was first settled in 1600.

Oldest European settlement

It's a relatively unassuming site today, but L'Anse aux Meadows at the northern tip of Newfoundland's Great Northern Peninsula is the oldest European settlement in the New World. Leif Erickson and crews of Norse explorers settled the spot in 1000 AD. The encampment was the source of myth and folklore until archaeologists discovered the site in 1968. In 1978, it was named a world heritage site by UNESCO.

Highest small city

The city of Kimberley, located in southeastern British Columbia, is the nation's highest small city (a population less than 100,000). It sits 1,110 m above sea level.

Highest big city

At an elevation of 1,048 m, Calgary is Canada's highest big city.

Highest town

Look up, way up — to Banff, Alberta, Canada's highest town. It sits at an elevation of 1,383 m above sea level.

Highest habitation

The hamlet of Lake Louise, Alberta, in Banff National Park, is the highest permanently inhabited place in Canada. It's located at 1,534 m above sea level.

Biggest convention centre

Looking for a place to show off? Try Toronto's Direct Energy Centre, the nation's largest convention and exhibition facility. Located at Exhibition Place, on the west side of the city's downtown, the centre boasts 99,592,000 square m of exhibit space in eight halls, plus the Ricoh Coliseum, an 8,200-seat arena.

Biggest geothermal mineral pool

Looking for natural relaxation? Try the Temple Gardens Mineral Spa Resort in Moose Jaw, Saskatchewan. It's home to the nation's largest therapeutic geothermal mineral water pool. The pool's waters are drawn from an ancient seabed more than 1,350 m underground and stay warm throughout the year.

Most historic downtown

Winnipeg's Exchange District, a national historic site, is considered one of the best preserved and largest collections of terra cotta and cut-stone architecture in North America. The 20-block area, the original core of Winnipeg, boasts about 150 heritage buildings, as well as a number of buildings that are national historic sites in their own right, including early skyscrapers.

Largest pedestrian walkway network

Calgary's +15 Skyway is a system of pedestrian walkways (including a series of elevated, protected bridges) that connect buildings in the city's downtown core. It is the largest network of its kind on Earth. Called the "+15" because it's about 15 feet above the ground, the 18 km system now has 62 bridges.

Most multicultural city

Talk about your united nations. Toronto is considered by many to be the most multicultural city in the world. More than 100 languages and dialects are spoken there.

Most immigrants

There's no doubt that Toronto is the Canada's most multicultural city. It's home to the largest percentage of immigrants in the country, with 37 percent of the nation's foreign-born residents, according to Statistics Canada. More than 2.5 million immigrants call Toronto home, making up 46 percent of the city's population.

Largest underground shopping complex

Your could call it the walkway to retail heaven. The PATH system in Toronto, an underground pathway that links 30 km of shops under a large portion of the city's downtown core, is considered the largest underground shopping complex in the world. PATH boasts 371,600 square m of retail space, houses about 1,200 shops and services, and connects more than 50 buildings.

Biggest historical reconstruction

The Fortress of Louisbourg, a national historic site located on Nova Scotia's Cape Breton Island, is the largest historical reconstruction in North America. First built in 1713 by the French, the settlement was besieged twice before being destroyed by the British in the 1760s. In 1961, the federal government committed $25 million to restore about one-quarter of the original village, which includes buildings, yards, gardens and streets, as well as part of the fortifications.

Largest living roof

The two-hectare "living roof" on the West Building of the Vancouver Convention Centre is the largest of its kind in Canada, and the largest non-industrial such roof in North America. Landscaped with more than 400,000 indigenous plants and grasses, the living roof helps insulate the building, keeping it cool in the summer and maintaining heat in the winter.

Biggest entertainment venue

Toronto's Exhibition Place is the nation's largest entertainment venue. The 77-hectare site is home to a variety of exhibition buildings, conference facilities and sporting venues, such as the Direct Energy Centre, the Better Living Centre, Ricoh Coliseum and BMO Field. It attracts more than 5.2 million visitors each year. Exhibition Place also hosts big events, including the Canadian National Exhibition and the Royal Winter Fair.

First lighthouse

It's no joke. The first documented lighthouse in Canada went into service on April 1, 1734, at Louisbourg, Nova Scotia. The stone tower was about 20 m tall and featured a fire chamber at the top fueled by coal. It was destroyed by the British in 1758, and today a modern lighthouse sits on the same location.

Longest downtown boardwalk

If you advance to this boardwalk, be prepared for a long walk. The Halifax Waterfront Boardwalk is the longest downtown boardwalk in the world. The 3.8 km trail runs from Pier 21 to Casino Nova Scotia and takes about 20 minutes to walk.

Oldest lighthouse

Cape Spear, Newfoundland, Canada's easternmost point, is home to the oldest surviving lighthouse in the province. Built in 1836, the Cape Spear Lighthouse is now a national historic site.

LAST WOODEN TIPPLE

The Atlas Coal Mine in Drumheller, Alberta, is home to the last wooden tipple — a structure used to load the coal from the mine into vehicles — in Canada. The mine shipped its last load of coal in 1979, bring an end to the coal era in that region.

Slurpee capital of the world

Winnipeg is famous for many things, but did you know it's considered the Slurpee Capital of the World? The crown is based on having the highest average number of Slurpee cups sold per store each year (400,000). The 7-Eleven store on Portage Avenue sell the second-most Slurpees in the country.

Biggest log cabin

Where else in the world would you find the globe's largest log cabin but in Canada? Specifically in Montebello, Quebec. Built in 1930 from 10,000 western red cedar logs and used as a private fishing lodge, the 211-room building is now the Fairmont Le Château Montebello.

Lobster capital of the world

It's hardly an officially designated title, but the town of Shediac, New Brunswick, lays claim to being the "Lobster Capital of the World." Shediac is home to lobster fishermen (naturally), processing plants, live tanks and the famous mid-July Lobster Festival.

Polar bear capital of the world

Churchill, Manitoba, is world renowned as the Polar Bear Capital of the World, thanks largely to its accessibility to the polar bear habitat. The bears can be seen through the summer, starting after mid-July, but it's not until October that the white bear's numbers really build. Through October and early November, it's possible to see 40 or more bears a day.

HIGHEST DAM

The highest dam in Canada is the Mica Dam in British Columbia, in operation since 1977. Located on the Columbia River, about 135 km from Revelstoke, the dam at the Mica Generating Station is 243 m high. The power plant accounts for 15 percent of the province's hydroelectric capacity.

Only walled city

Quebec City is the only walled city in North America and the oldest city on the continent north of the Mexico border. It was founded in 1608. The Historic District of Old Quebec is a UNESCO world heritage site, the first city in North America to receive the designation.

BIGGEST ARCH AND BUTTRESS DAM

Quebec's Daniel-Johnston Dam, located on the Manicouagan River some 200 km north of Baie-Comeau, is the world's largest multiple arch and buttress dam. The 214 m high dam, which was completed in 1968, boasts 14 buttresses across its 1,310 m length.

One city, two provinces

Here's a unique geographical distinction: Lloydminster is the only city in Canada that straddles a provincial border. Located almost the same distance from both Edmonton and Saskatoon, Lloydminster was first settled in 1903. When the provinces of Alberta and Saskatchewan were formed in 1905, the settlement was split along the 4th meridian, the provincial boundary. On May 20, 1930, the two communities were reunited as a single municipality.

Biggest stock exchange

The Toronto Stock Exchange is the largest stock exchange in Canada, the third-largest in North America and the seventh-largest in the world. It opened on October 25, 1861, and 18 stocks could be traded. The TSE became a publically traded company in 2000 (two years later adopting the abbreviation TSX). In 2008 it acquired the Montreal Exchange.

TSE firsts

The Toronto Stock Exchange has been a world leader. In 1977, the TSE was the world's first stock exchange to introduce computer-assisted trading, and in the late 1990s it was the first exchange to introduce decimal trading (as opposed to fractions). It was the largest North American exchange to rely completely on electronic trading and the first to have a female president, Barbara G. Stymiest.

Oldest company

The Hudson's Bay Company, founded in 1670, is North America's oldest continuously operating company. In its earliest days, the business was instrumental in European development in the country, particularly its eastern half, where numerous outposts were set up to trade goods. Today, HBC runs the country's largest department store, with 90 locations across the nation.

Biggest uranium producer

Canada is the globe's largest producer of uranium, accounting for 18 percent of the world's production of the element. (Uranium is processed to create fuel for nuclear reactors.)

Biggest uranium mine

Saskatchewan's McArthur River mine is the largest high-grade uranium mine on Earth. It can produce more than 8.16 million kg of uranium each year by mining just 150 to 200 tonnes of ore per day.

First Hudson's Bay blankets

The first of the now-famous, classic Hudson's Bay Company point blankets, known for their bands of colour, were shipped to HBC posts on a regular basis in the spring of 1780.

Biggest ammolite mine

Canada is home to the world's largest ammolite mine. The Ammolite Mine near Lethbridge, Alberta, produces more than 90 percent of the global supply of the rare multicoloured gemstone.

Richest vein of silver

The world's richest vein of silver was found in Cobalt, Ontario in 1903. In the following 60 years, silver mines in the area produced a total of almost 1.2 million tonnes of silver ore and concentrates, and the total production over that time was more than 11,921 million g of silver. The silver rush ended somewhat abruptly in the mid-20th century, and the town turned its mining attention to the mineral it was named after. Thanks to improved technology, cobalt had become more useful.

Biggest zinc producer

Canada is one of the world's largest producers of zinc. Zinc is primarily used to galvanize steel against corrosion. The Teck Trail Operation in British Columbia is one of the world's largest, highest-margin, fully integrated zinc and lead smelting and refining operations.

553 m

Mancassa gold mine: 2,200 m deep

Deepest

That's one deep hole. The Macassa gold mine in Kirkland Lake, Ontario, is the deepest mine shaft in Canada, at 2,200 m. Until the mid-1990s, it was the deepest shaft in the Western Hemisphere). Operations at the Macassa mine closed down in 1999.

Biggest diamond mine

Canada's largest diamond mine, Diavik, is located 300 km north of Yellowknife, Northwest Territories. Run as part of the Rio Tinto group of companies, the reserves are located in three diamond ore bodies. Since production began in 2003, more than 50 million carats of rough diamonds have been extracted.

Oldest mines

The oldest operating mines in Canada are the Stobie Mine and the Copper Cliff North Mine near Sudbury, Ontario. Both mines began operation in 1886.

Biggest gold rush

The biggest gold rush in Canadian history was the Klondike Gold Rush from 1897 to 1899. During that time, 40,000 fortune seekers made their way to gold fields near Dawson, Yukon. By the end of the rush, prospectors spent an estimated $50 million reaching the Klondike, an amount essentially equal to the value of the gold extracted during those years.

Northernmost mine

The planet's northernmost mine was the Polaris lead and zinc mine on Little Cornwallis Island in Nunavut. Before it closed in 2002, more than one million tonnes of ore were extracted annually. Its operators undertook 22 years of exploration before opening the mine in 1981. Along with the nearby Nanisivik lead and zinc mine, Polaris was one of the lowest-cost producers of zinc on the planet and made Nunavut the largest producer of zinc in Canada.

Biggest mining province

When it comes to mining in Canada, images of the Yukon gold rush come to mind. Ontario, however, is the country's leading metal producer. Twenty-five different metal and non-metal mineral products are produced in the province, including 43 percent of the nation's nickel, 52 percent of its gold, 38 percent of copper and 84 percent of platinum metals.

Biggest salt mine

Need salt for that? Then head to Goderich, Ontario, home of the world's largest salt mine. Owned by Sifto Canada, 6,577,089 tonnes of salt are mined from the site every year.

FIRST OIL COMPANY

Oil! The first oil company in North America was founded in the aptly named community of Oil Springs, Ontario, southeast of Sarnia. On December 18, 1854, Charles Tripp received approval for his commercial oil company.

Biggest mustard producer

If you like your mustard, thank Saskatchewan. The prairie province is the world's largest mustard exporter. In 2013, the province produced 117,000 tonnes of mustard in three different types — yellow, brown and oriental.

Biggest towed object

The Hibernia oil platform, located in the waters of the Grand Banks off Newfoundland, is believed to be the largest object ever towed. It took 13 days — from May 23 to June 5, 1997 — to tow the 1.08 million tonne structure from Bull Arm, Newfoundland, to the Grand Banks.

Biggest wheat-producing province

Saskatchewan grows 45 percent of Canada's grain. It also produces more than 54 percent of the nation's wheat. Its production also accounts for 10 percent of the world's total exported wheat.

Biggest flaxseed producer

Canada is well known as a producer of a number of agricultural crops. Among them is flaxseed, and Canada is the world's largest producer, accounting for 40 percent of global production. Flaxseed is principally grown on the prairies and used for linseed oil, which is used as a drying oil in paints and varnish and in the production of linoleum and printing inks.

Biggest fertilizer company

You could say it's a growing business. PotashCorp, based in Saskatoon, Saskatchewan, is the world's largest fertilizer company by capacity. It produces fertilizers from potash, phosphate and nitrogen. The company is aptly named, as it's the global leader in potash production, with 20 percent of the global capacity coming from its Canadian operations.

Best farmland

Think of farming in Canada and you probably think of the prairies or Prince Edward Island potatoes. But Ontario has more than half of the nation's "Class 1" agricultural land (the highest quality farming property). The province's 51,950 farms contribute almost one-quarter of the country's farm revenue.

First grain distillery

John Molson opened the nation's first industrial grain distillery. The Molson distillery became the first exporter of Canadian-made spirits to England, and it was the country's largest distillery until it closed in 1866.

OLDEST BREWERY

Canada is home to the oldest brewery in North America. Molson was established in Montreal in 1786 by John Molson. The Molson brand is the oldest beer brand on the continent.

First winery

Canada's first commercial winery was established in 1866 in Pelee Island, Ontario, the nation's most-southerly point of land. It was founded by a group of farmers from Kentucky, who planted 12 hectares of native North American Catawba grapes to produce the beverage.

Most pulp-and-paper

Pulp-and-paper production is the largest manufacturing industry in Canada (pictured is a factory in Cornerbrook, Newfoundland). The nation has about 140 pulp, pulp-and-paper, and paper mills, and employs some 85,000 people.

Most French fries

Get out the ketchup. And lots of it. McCain Foods, whose global headquarters is located in Florenceville-Bristol, New Brunswick, is the world's largest manufacturer of French fries. Indeed, one of every three French fries eaten on Earth is a McCain fry.

Most maple syrup

Canada is the world's leading producer of maple syrup (the United States is the only other country to produce it). Canada produces 82 percent of the globe's maple syrup, valued at more than $177 million. More than 90 percent of Canadian maple syrup comes from Quebec. About 83 percent of the syrup produced in Canada is exported.

Most lumber

Not only does Canada lead the world as an exporter of softwood lumber, but British Columbia is the global export leader of the product. The province moves out more than 11.3 million cubic m of softwood, worth close to $11 million. The United States, China and Japan are the three largest importers of the wood.

Most newsprint

With all that tree-covered hinterland, is it any wonder that Canada is the world's largest exporter of market pulp and newsprint? The forestry industry contributes up to three percent of the nation's gross domestic product; more than $34 billion in forest products are exported annually.

First paper mill

Canada's first paper mill was established in 1805 in St. Andrews, Quebec. It created printing, writing and wrapping papers for markets in Montreal and Quebec City.

Most common cow

The Holstein is the most common dairy cow breed in Canada, accounting for 94 percent of the country's cows.

Biggest hydroelectric development

The biggest hydroelectric power development in Canada is Quebec's James Bay Project (pictured is its expansion in 1990). It started producing electricity in 1982. Its eight dams and 198 dikes contain five reservoirs covering 11,900 square km, half the size of Lake Ontario. The combined output of its generating stations is 10,283 megawatts.

First hydroelectric transmission

The Barber Paper Mill of Georgetown, Ontario, has a powerful place in the country's history. In 1888, the mill's John R. Barber commissioned the Cleveland Brush Company to build a 60 hp motor and a 100 hp generator for him. He built a power plant called the "Dynamo," which transmitted power from a dam on the Credit River to the mill three km away. This is believed to be the first transmission of hydroelectric power over a distance in North America.

Most manufacturing

Ontario is considered part of the manufacturing heartland of North America. The province has more manufacturing employees than anywhere else in Canada and ranks third in North America to California and Texas.

First tidal power plant

The first tidal power plant in the Americas, and the only one in North America, was built near Annapolis Royal, Nova Scotia, in 1984. The Annapolis Tidal Station has a capacity of 20 megawatts, and depending on the tides, a daily output of roughly 80 to 100 megawatt hours. It boasts the world's largest straight-flow turbine generator, capable of producing more than 30 million kilowatt hours of electricity per year, enough to power some 4,500 homes.

Most cars

When it comes to cars, there's a good chance it comes from Ontario. The province is the largest regional automotive assembly jurisdiction in North America. In 2011, Statistics Canada reports that 88 percent of the province's vehicle production was exported, almost entirely to the United States.

First publically owned utility

In 1906, the Ontario government created the world's first publically owned utility, the Hydro-Electric Power Commission of Ontario. Its primary goal was to build transmission lines to supply southern Ontario with power generated in Niagara Falls by existing private companies.

Most wind power

Boasting more than 1,000 wind turbines with a capacity of more than 2,000 megawatts, Ontario is the nation's leader in wind-power production.

Biggest airline

It serves a customer base as large as the country's population. Air Canada is the nation's largest full-service airline. The company moves 35 million passengers each year to more than 175 destinations around the world.

Largest youth employer

Help wanted. Canada's Wonderland, the nation's largest amusement park, located just north of Toronto, is the single largest employer of youth in Canada. It's also the top employer in York Region, the municipality where it's located. The park employs more than 4,000 seasonal staff.

Biggest hotel

Toronto's Eaton Chelsea is the country's largest hotel. It boasts 1,590 guestrooms and more than 2,200 square m of meeting and event space, including two ballrooms. The hotel also has four dining options.

TRANSMISSION LINES

First 50-kilovolt

North America's first high-voltage (50-kilovolt) transmission line was installed in 1903. It carried electricity 136 km, from the Shawinigan Water and Power Company to aluminum and pulp-and-paper manufacturers in Montreal.

First 100-kilovolt

In 1910, the Hydro-Electric Power Commission of Ontario built the first 100-kilovolt transmission line. The line ran from Niagara Falls to power a number of communities in southern Ontario, including Toronto.

First 220-kilovolt

In 1928, the first 220-kilovolt transmission line ran from Paugan Falls, Quebec, to Toronto, a distance of more than 440 km.

First 360-kilovolt

The first 360-kilovolt transmission line was built by B.C. Electric in 1963.

First 735-kilovolt

Danger: high voltage! Hydro-Quebec developed the world's first commercial 735-kilovolt power transmission line, along with the earliest equipment designed for the high voltage. It was commissioned in 1965 to link the Manic-Outardes generating stations to Montreal and Quebec.

Biggest solar farm

The Sarnia Solar Project in Sarnia, Ontario, is the country's largest solar farm. The facility boasts 1.3 million individual solar modules, which combined are capable of producing 80 megawatts of electricity, or enough to power 10,000 homes annually. This saves about 22 tonnes of carbon dioxide emissions each year.

Highest gross domestic product

Further bolstering Calgary's rise as one of the country's financial centres is the fact that the city has had the highest total gross domestic product in Canada over the past 10 years (from 2001 to 2010), at 29.6 percent.

Fastest growth

Calgary is growing by leaps and bounds and leads the nation in average 10-year growth rate for major cities (from 2001 to 2010). It's grown by 2.9 percent in that time.

Largest grocery chain

Grab a grocery cart. Loblaw Companies Limited is the country's largest food retailer, attracting more than 14 million shoppers to its stores every week. It operates more than 1,000 stores across the country, including Loblaws, Independent, Valu-mart, Zehrs, No Frills, Real Canadian Superstore, Maxi, SaveEasy and Extra Foods.

Most head offices

Despite being considered the country's financial capital, Toronto does not lead the nation in number of head offices. Calgary holds the distinction of the highest concentration of head offices per capita in Canada, at 9.3 percent.

Biggest bulk food store

Bulk Barn is Canada's largest bulk food retailer. First opened in 1982, the company now has more than 200 locations across the country. Bulk Barn offers more than 4,000 products, everything from nuts and spices to pet food.

Oldest chartered bank

If you're looking for a Canadian financial institution with a long history, look no further than the Bank of Montreal, the nation's oldest chartered bank. Established in 1871, it served as the banker for the Canadian government from 1863 until 1935, when the Bank of Canada was formed.

First international bank

The Bank of Montreal was the first Canadian financial institution to have agencies beyond the country's borders. In 1818 it established representatives in London and New York.

First credit union

The first credit union in North America, La Caisse Populaire de Levis, was established in 1900 in Levis, Quebec, by journalist Alphonse Desjardins. Nine years later, Desjardins helped organize the first credit union in the United States, the St. Mary's Cooperative Credit Association.

Largest chocolate seller

Laura Secord, the chocolate company formed in 1913, is the nation's largest chocolatier. Today the company boasts more than 120 stores across the country and more than 400 products.

HIGHEST WAGES

Want to make some serious salary? Calgary's the place to be for that. It leads the nation in highest wages and salaries per employee for a decade (2001 to 2010). In 2010, the average wage per employee was $65,121.

Biggest Creative Output

Ontario is the country's hotbed of creativity, at least when it comes to its entertainment and publishing industries, which are the largest in Canada and the third-largest in North America (after California and New York). Ontario leads the nation in film and television production, book and magazine publishing and sound recording.

Oldest farmers' market

The oldest farmers' market in Canada is the Halifax Farmers' Market, which was created by royal proclamation in June 1750, a year after the city was founded. Known today as the Halifax Seaport Farmers' Market, it is also the longest-running farmers' market in North America. Nowadays it hosts more than 250 vendors.

MOST CATERPILLARS

Finning International, headquartered in Vancouver, is the world's largest dealer of Caterpillar products, which include construction and mining equipment vehicles. Finning sells and rents the Cat equipment to mining, construction, oil and gas, and forestry industries around the world. In 2012 the company generated $3.3 billion in revenue.

First stratospheric balloon

In September 2013, the Canadian Space Agency, in partnership with the French space agency (Centre national d'études spatiales), completed the first launch of a stratospheric research balloon in Canada. The remote-controlled balloon was launched from Timmins, Ontario. It can haul up to 1.58 tonnes of equipment, requires no fuel and is fully recoverable.

Biggest farmers' market

With a population of only about 2,000, it's hard to believe that St. Jacobs, Ontario, located west of Toronto, is the home of the nation's largest year-round farmers' market. Approximately 4,000 Old Order Mennonites from the surrounding area are key to the market's size and success. Open Thursdays and Saturdays, the market has hundreds of vendors.

First coin

The first domestically produced Canadian coin was struck on January 2, 1908, at the opening ceremony for the Royal Mint in Ottawa. The silver 50-cent piece bore the effigy of King Edward VII.

Pure gold coin (1)

In 1982, the Royal Canadian Mint's refinery produced the world's first 9999 (99.9 percent pure) gold bullion coins — the Gold Maple Leaf coin.

Pure gold coin (2)

In 2007, the Royal Canadian Mint one-upped itself by producing the world's first 99999 (99.999 percent pure) gold bullion coin. It is the only mint in the world to produce coins at this standard.

First $1 million coin

Don't try making change for this coin. The Royal Canadian Mint created the world's first $1 million coin in 2007. The 100 kg, 99999 (99.999 percent) pure gold bullion coin was created to market the Mint's new standard for gold coin purity. However, a number of people came forward interested in purchasing the real McCoy. The Mint has subsequently sold five of the colossal coins, which at the time were the world's largest.

THE
QUEBEC
GAZETTE

THURSDAY, APRIL 19, 1804.

Magazine with largest circulation

Maclean's has the largest circulation of any weekly magazine in Canada. Each of the publication's 44 issues per year are circulated to more than 310,000 people. The magazine reaches an estimated 2.4 million readers.

First bilingual newspaper

Canada's first bilingual newspaper, *The Quebec Gazette*, was based in Quebec City and was established in 1764 by two Philadelphia printers, William Brown and Thomas Gilmore.

Newspaper with the most readers

The *Toronto Star* is the nation's largest daily newspaper. Established as *The Evening Star* on November 3, 1892, the paper now has more than three million readers every week (in print and online). Its weekday editions are circulated to nearly 350,000 people, while its Saturday paper reaches more than 470,000 readers.

First newspaper

It was a humble beginning, but an important one. Printed on half a foolscap sheet, Canada's first newspaper debuted on March 23, 1752. The day's edition of the *Halifax Gazette* boasted news from Europe, Britain and the other British colonies to the south.

First daily newspaper

The *Montreal Daily Advertiser*, established in 1883, was the nation's first daily newspaper. It went bankrupt within a year of its first edition.

Biggest publisher

Rogers Publishing, a division of Rogers Media, is the nation's largest publisher. It produces both consumer and industry magazines, including well known Canadian titles such as *Maclean's*, *Chatelaine*, *Flare*, *Hello! Canada*, *Canadian Business* and *L'actualité*. In all, it publishes some 75,000 magazine pages annually.

Oldest student publication

Toronto's Upper Canada College private school is home to the nation's oldest continuously running student publication. The *College Times* has been published since 1871.

Most romance

Harlequin Romance, one of the world's leading publishers of books for women (it has sold an estimated 6.28 billion books since its inception), was founded in May 1949 in Winnipeg. In 1969, the company relocated to Toronto, where today it publishes more than 110 titles a month in 34 languages, which are sold in 110 countries on six continents.

Oldest continuously published newspaper

The Montreal Gazette is the nation's oldest continuously operating newspaper and one of the oldest in North America. Founded by Fleury Mesplet as a French paper in 1778, the paper became bilingual in the late 1700s, then changed to English-only in 1822. Today, *The Gazette* is the dominant newspaper for reaching English speakers in Montreal.

First newspaper published by a black woman

Mary Ann Shadd was the first black woman in North America to publish a newspaper, the *Provincial Freeman*, which she established in 1853 in Windsor, Ontario, and later published in Toronto and Chatham, Ontario. The paper provided information about the successes of black people living in freedom in Canada. Shadd herself had emigrated to Canada from the United States.

OLDEST NEWSPAPER IN ONTARIO

The *Kingston Whig-Standard* of Kingston, Ontario, is Canada's oldest continually published daily newspaper. It was first established in March 1810 as the *Kingston Gazette* and adopted its present moniker in 1849.

Oldest magazine

Based in Toronto, the *United Church Observer* is the oldest continuously published magazine in North America, and the second oldest continuously published English-language magazine in the world. It was established in 1829 as the *Christian Guardian* and has had several name changes since then.

First phone call

Alexander Graham Bell was a man of many firsts, not the least of which was making the first one-way, long-distance telephone calls between the Ontario communities of Brantford and Paris, and Mount Pleasant and Brantford, on August 10, 1876. Bell received that first call from Brantford in Robert White's Boot and Shoe Store and Telegram Office in Paris.

First trans-Canada telephone system

The first "trans-Canada" telephone system was completed in 1932. It covered Toronto, Montreal, Quebec City, Hamilton and Windsor.

First radio message

It's an apt name. Signal Hill in St. John's, Newfoundland, was the site where the first transatlantic radio telegraphic message was received, by Guglielmo Marconi on December 12, 1901. Marconi used an antenna raised by a kite to transmit and receive that first Morse-code message. The Tower at Signal Hill, now part of a national historic site, was used for signalling until 1960.

First microwave voice transmission system

The world's first commercial microwave relay system for voice transmissions was installed between Nova Scotia and Prince Edward Island on November 19, 1948, ending the need for underwater cables.

First telegraph

Oh how far we've come. The first electric telegraph message sent in Canada was from Toronto to Hamilton on December 19, 1846. The early means of electronically sending encoded messages was sent between Toronto City Hall and Hamilton on a line owned by the Toronto, Hamilton and Niagara Electric-Magnetic Telegraph Company. The transmission: "Advise Mr. Gamble [president of the telegraph company] that Mr. Dawson will speak to him at half-past one."

First emergency number

Who doesn't know the phone number 911 and what it's for? But did you know that Winnipeg was the first city in North America to implement a central phone number to contact emergency services? The number (the city used 999 at the time) was introduced on June 21, 1959, at the suggestion of Winnipeg mayor Stephen Juba. Most of North America adopted 911 as the emergency contact number on June 22, 1975.

First submarine telegraph cable

The first submarine telegraph cable in North America was laid by Frederick N. Gisborne between New Brunswick and Prince Edward Island in 1852, most of it by a machine he devised himself. He also engineered the first link between Cape Breton and Cape Ray, Newfoundland, in

First transatlantic telephone cable

A cooperative effort of the General Post Office of the United Kingdom, American Telegraph and Telephone and the Canadian Overseas Telephone Corporation, TAT-1 was the first transatlantic telephone cable. Actually there were two cables, laid side by side (one running in each direction) in the summer of 1955 and 1956. TAT-1 linked Scotland near Oban to London and to Clarenville, Newfoundland, then across the Cabot Strait to Nova Scotia.

First commercial radio station

The first commercial radio station in Canada, and some argue, in the world, was XWA Montreal (subsequently known as CFCF, CIQC and AM940). It hit the airwaves in 1919. The first broadcast: "Hello! Hello! This is wireless telephone station XWA at Montreal. Hello! Hello! How are you getting this? Is it clear? Is the modulation okay? XWA at Montreal is changing over." The station stopped broadcasting in January 2010.

First trans-Canada broadcast

It was a special Canada Day. On July 1, 1927, Prime Minister Mackenzie King spoke to Canadians from Parliament Hill in the first trans-Canada radio broadcast. The milestone event included a variety of other speeches and performances in recognition of the Diamond Jubilee of Canada's Confederation.

First music and voice radio broadcast

Seems as though the impression that all the top musical acts on the radio are Canadian isn't so new. Canadian inventor Reginald Fessenden, born in Knowlton, Quebec, made the first public broadcast of music and voice on December 24, 1906. The broadcast, from Fessenden's headquarters in Brant Rock, Massachusetts, included a Bible passage, a phonograph recording of Handel and a performance of "O Holy Night" on the violin by Fessenden himself.

First voice radio transmission

Reginald Fessenden (see **First music and voice radio broadcast, left**) is also credited with the first achievement in the creation of what is now radio. On December 23, 1900, he sent the world's first wireless transmission of a human voice at Cobb Island, Maryland. The signal, sent via electromagnetic waves, travelled about 1.5 km.

First French radio station

Montreal's CKAC was the first French-language radio station in Canada. It was inaugurated on September 27, 1922.

First television broadcast

The first television pictures in Canada were broadcast in the summer of 1932, using the CKAC radio transmission in Montreal. The broadcasts were experimental and only a handful of people had receivers to view them on. In October 1932, Canadian Television Ltd. held a public demonstration of the technology at Montreal's Ogilvy department store, which was attended by thousands.

First television weather report

Doesn't it figure that the first broadcast on Canadian television would include a weather update? Canada's first television station, CBC's CBFT Montreal, debuted on September 6, 1952. The first broadcast included the flickering test pattern of an Indian surrounded by a geometric design (broadcast upside down!), followed by a news item on two men who had just robbed a bank, a puppet show (*Uncle Chichimus*), and then, finally, a weather report with meteorologist Percy

First televised question period

The CBC began to broadcast question period from the House of Commons live for the first time in 1977. In the first few weeks of broadcasts, several MPs wore sunglasses to avoid the bright television lights.

First televised debate

The first televised debate by leaders of political parties in Canada (involving Tommy Douglas, Pierre Trudeau, Robert Stanfield and Réal Caouette) took place on June 9, 1968.

First television satellite

Launched on January 17, 1976, *Hermes*, a collaborative effort between Canada and the United States, was the first satellite to broadcast television signals into homes. The most powerful satellite at the time, *Hermes* demonstrated direct broadcasting to Peru, Australia and Papua New Guinea, in addition to experiments conducted in Canada and the United States.

Third nation in space

Canada became the third nation in space — after the United States and the U.S.S.R. — on September 29, 1962, with the launch of the research satellite *Alouette-I*. Designed to last for one year, the satellite ultimately performed flawlessly for 10 years.

First text message

It figures a twenty-something was the first person to send a text message. What's not so predictable is that the British man who sent it now lives in Montreal. At 22 years old, Neil Papworth typed out the short note that would spawn a new form of communication on December 3, 1992. At the time he was an employee at Sema, a software company in England, and his message was brief, but seasonal: "Merry Christmas."

LONGEST FIBRE-OPTICS NETWORK

SaskTel, a communications company based in Regina, created the world's longest commercial fibre-optics network, which was completed in 1984. The 3,268 km network connected 52 of the province's largest communities.

First Earth observation satellite

The first high-resolution satellite image ever taken of the South Pole was captured in 1997 from Canada's first Earth observation satellite system, RADARSAT-1. Launched on November 4, 1995, RADARSAT-1 was capable of acquiring images of Earth in any conditions, day or night, rain or shine.

First communications satellite

The Anik A1 was the world's first domestic geostationary communications satellite system. It was launched on November 9, 1972. The system enabled Telesat Canada to provide high-quality telephone service to Canada's north and television service across the country.

Frozen Food

If you're a fan of fish sticks — or any frozen food for that matter — you can thank marine scientist Archibald Huntsman. In 1926, while working for the Biological Board of Canada (later the Fisheries Research Board) in Halifax, Huntsman began work on developing a commercial frozen fish product. The result? Ice Fillets debuted in 1929 in Toronto, marking the first time frozen food was sold to the public. The product was pricey, but popular. Unfortunately, fishing companies lost interest, and the Ice Fillets were abandoned in 1931.

McIntosh apple

If apple pie is a traditional American dish, the McIntosh apple is as Canadian as it gets. In 1811, John McIntosh discovered an apple sapling on his farm near Dundela, Ontario, which subsequently produced a fruit with a great taste, texture, aroma and appearance. It was also ideally suited for growing in Canada's colder climate. John's son Allan established a nursery for the species and promoted it widely. It has since become one of the most popular apple varieties in Canada and around the world.

Spartan apple

Here's another great Canadian food invention: the Spartan apple. The variety was first developed in Summerland, British Columbia, by R.C. Palmer at a federal experimental farm. Interestingly, the exact parentage of the species is in question. It was once thought to be a cross between a McIntosh and a Newtown, but testing has ruled out the Newtown.

Pablum

The nutritious baby food, Pablum, was created in 1930 by Alan Brown, Theo Drake and Fred Tisdall, to help prevent and treat rickets in children. The popular product improved the health of millions of children around the world and led to ideas for a number of other nutritious foods for infants. The three doctors at Toronto's Sick Kids Hospital donated royalties from the product back to the hospital.

Canola

Its name kind of gives it away. Canola, the globe's only made-in-Canada crop, was created in the 1970s by researchers from Agriculture and Agri-Food Canada and the University of Manitoba. Today, canola is considered one of the most important oilseed crops in the world and has proved to be the most lucrative for Canadian farmers. Vegetable oil made from canola plant seeds also lays claim to being the healthiest vegetable oil on the planet.

OLDEST CANDY COMPANY

If you're a Canadian candy connoisseur, you'll appreciate this. Ganong Bros. Limited of St. Stephen, New Brunswick, is Canada's oldest candy company. It was established in 1873. The business is responsible for a number of candy firsts: the first Canadian lollipop in 1895; the first chocolate nut bar in North America in 1910; the first heart-shaped box for chocolates (introduced originally for Christmas) in 1932; and the first fruit snack made from real fruit in purée form, in 1988.

Red Fife wheat

Canadian wheat is known as some of the finest in the world. The oldest of the nation's wheat varieties is Red Fife, which was first grown in Peterborough, Ontario on the farm of Dave Fife in 1842. Red Fife was known as a fine milling and baking wheat, and by the 1860s it was being cultivated across the nation. Red Fife was considered the country's wheat standard for more than four decades, from about 1860 to 1900.

Marquis wheat

In the early 1900s, a Canadian produced wheat called Marquis replaced Red Fife as the nation's top wheat. It was a cross between Red Fife and Hard Red Calcutta. Marquis matured seven to 10 days earlier than Red Fife and produced a great yield of 41.6 bushels per acre, while retaining the baking quality of Fife. The yield and quality of Marquis made Canada the largest wheat-exporting nation on the planet.

Bloody Caesar

The Bloody Caesar cocktail was first created in 1969 at Marco's Italian restaurant at the Calgary Inn (which is now the Westin Calgary). The beverage was invented to celebrate the restaurant's grand opening.

Yukon Gold potato

The Yukon Gold potato naturally was created in Canada. Bred at the University of Guelph in 1966, the Yukon Gold is known for its longevity in storage, as well as being a very good potato for baking, boiling and French frying. It was released to market in 1981.

Best potato for French fries

If you eat French fries, there's a good chance you've eaten a Canadian food innovation. The Shepody potato, released by Agri-Food Canada's research lab in Fredericton, New Brunswick, in 1983, quickly became one of the world's most popular potatoes for French fries. The Shepody is known for its short growing season and high yields.

Peanut butter

Here's something nutty: Montreal's Marcellus Gilmore Edson was the first person to patent modern peanut butter in 1884.

Canada Dry ginger ale

You knew this! Canada Dry ginger ale was created in Canada, by Toronto chemist and pharmacist John J. McLaughlin. He's said to have perfected the recipe in 1904.

Sugar-free pop and popcans

A couple more firsts for the pop industry from the makers of Canada Dry: During the 1950s and 1960s, the company was the first of the major soft drink makers to market sugar-free beverages, and the first to put pop in cans.

INNOVATIONS

Robertson screwdriver

What do you do when you screw up? Invent a new screwdriver. After cutting his hand using a spring-loaded screwdriver in Montreal, Peter Lymburner Robertson decided to improve the tool. The result: the Robertson Drive screwdriver, which was patented in 1909. The square-headed driver and screw could be driven more quickly and reduced the slipping common with other screwdrivers.

Paint roller

It's oh, so simple! And saves countless backbreaking hours of work. Plus, it's hardly changed in more than 80 years: the paint roller. It was invented by Norman Breakey of Toronto in 1940. Unfortunately, Breakey never got to roll in the profits, as he was never able to make enough rollers to profit from it before competitors made slightly different variations and sold it as their own invention.

First Canadian stamp

In 1851, the first Canadian postage stamp, the Three-Pence Beaver, was designed by Sir Sandford Fleming. The design was one of the first in the world to feature a pictorial, as opposed to a portrait of a monarch, a statesman, a geometric design or a coat-of-arms. The first of these stamps was issued on April 23 of that year.

Green plastic garbage bag

Three Canadians lay claim to the invention of an indispensible household product: the green plastic garbage bag. Harry Wasyluk of Winnipeg, Larry Hanson at Union Carbide in Lindsay, Ontario, and Frank Plomp of Toronto all came up with variations of the polyethylene bags in the 1950s, which were originally sold to hospitals and businesses.

First light bulb

Thomas Edison gets all the recognition, but a Toronto medical student named Henry Woodward, with help from a city innkeeper named Matthew Evans, developed and patented a predecessor to Edison's light bulb in 1874. The duo didn't have the money to produce and sell the bulbs, and sold the patent in 1875 to Edison. His light bulb debuted in 1879.

Acetylene gas

Here's another bright idea. Electrical engineer Thomas Wilson, who was born in Princeton, Ontario, developed the first commercial process to produce calcium carbide, a chemical used to make acetylene gas, in 1892. At the turn of the 20th century, acetylene gas was widely used for lighting.

Kerosene

Abraham Gesner of Cornwallis, Nova Scotia, is the inventor of kerosene. The geologist started experiments to distill oil in the form of kerosene in 1846, and had created the lamp oil by 1853. Around that time, the fuel became the lighting standard in homes. Thanks to his patents for distilling bituminuous materials, Gesner is also considered a founder of the modern petroleum industry.

Snowmobile

While there were patents for snowmobiles that pre-dated his, Joseph-Armand Bombardier is widely considered the inventor of the modern-day snowmobile. Born in Sherbrooke, Quebec, on April 16, 1907, Bombardier invented his first snowmobile in 1937, which was successful largely because of the front steering skis and the rear tracked drive. In 1959, Bombardier debuted the Ski-Doo® Snowmobile, the motorcycle-sized version of his original invention.

Snow blower

This is hardly a surprise. The snow blower was invented by Canadian Arthur Sicard, born in Saint-Leonard-de-Port-Maurice, Quebec, in 1925. He sold the first commercial self-propelled rotary machine in 1927. The blower was made of a four-wheel-drive truck chassis, a truck motor, a snow-blower head with two adjustable chutes and another motor to drive the snow-blower head.

Ski-Doo® is a trademark of BRP.

Artificial fur

A Canadian project during the Second World War to develop better Arctic clothing for the military led to the first patent for artificial fur.

Snowplow

What else would a Canadian dentist invent, but the first rotary snowplow? Huh? Indeed, Toronto's Dr. J.W. Elliot invented the machine in 1869. But one was never built until the winter of 1883–84 after another Canadian, Orange Jull, improved on the original design. Designed for trains, the invention became standard on trains through the winter.

Foghorn

Spend any amount of time in the Maritimes and you'll see a lot of fog. So is it any wonder the world's first steam-operated foghorn was invented in New Brunswick? In 1854, after first-hand experience with the Bay of Fundy fog, Robert Foulis invented the device. The first was installed on the province's Partridge Island in 1859. Nations around the globe subsequently adopted the use of the horn.

Halftone photographic printing

Canadians Georges-Édouard Desbarats and William Leggo (pictured here) are credited with the invention of halftone photographic printing. The process was first unveiled in print in 1869 in the *Canadian Illustrated News*, a publication Desbarats had founded.

Anti-torpedo gear

The Canadian Anti-Acoustic Torpedo (CAT) gear was created during the Second World War. This was a countermeasure to acoustic torpedoes and was deployed on a cable near the ship to deflect an attack. CAT is credited with saving many ships from torpedoes.

Panoramic camera

Talk about taking a wide-angled view of the world! Canadian John R. Connon patented the panoramic camera in 1888. Although there are earlier patents for similar devices, Connon's was the first to capture vistas of up to 360 degrees in a single exposure.

Portable film-developing tank

In 1899, Nova Scotian Arthur Williams McCurdy invented a small portable tank for developing film in daytime, called the Ededec, which was used by photographers for generations. After patenting the device in the United States in 1902, McCurdy sold it to the Eastman Kodak company.

Walkie-talkie

Canadian Donald L. Hings invented the walkie-talkie in 1937. The first versions of the device were designed as portable radios for bush pilots working for Consolidated Mining and Smelting (now Cominco), where Hings was employed. It wasn't until the Second World War, when the company lent Hings to the Department of National Defence and the National Research Council, that the walkie-talkie became widely used.

Degaussing process

Sir Charles Goodeve, born in Neepawa, Manitoba, on February 21, 1904, invented the process of degaussing in 1940, which helped protect ships from magnetic mines by reducing the hull's magnetism.

Short-wave transmitter

Installed in Drummondville, Quebec, in 1926, the Drummondville transmitter was the first short-wave link between England and Canada. At first it only transmitted Morse code, but eventually was modified to carry voice as well.

Batteryless radio

The Rogers batteryless receiver, created by E.S. Ted Rogers, was unveiled at Toronto's Canadian National Exhibition in 1925. The radio was one of the first successful batteryless sets on the market.

FATHOMETER

Canadian Reginald Fessenden created the fathometer, a device that measured the depth of water under a ship's hull. The invention won him *Scientific American*'s Gold Medal in 1929.

Gas mask

There's a saying that necessity is the mother of invention. This may never have been more true than when it came to the invention of the first military gas mask, which was invented by Dr. Cluny Macpherson of St. John's in 1915. Macpherson attached a canvas hood with eyeholes and a breathing tube to a helmet that had been treated with chemicals to absorb chlorine used in German gas attacks.

Painted road lines

Sometimes you just have to draw a line. Indeed, in the 1930s, engineer John D. Millar of the Ontario Department of Transport came up with the idea of painting lines on roads to ensure traffic stayed in its own lane. The world's first road lines were painted on a stretch of highway near the Ontario-Quebec border, and within three years the lines were commonplace throughout the continent.

Jolly Jumper

The Jolly Jumper, the device designed for infants, was invented by Canadian Susan Olivia Poole in 1910. The original was made for Poole's first child Joseph. It wasn't until 1948—and after all seven of Poole's children had used the device—that the Jolly Jumper was mass-produced for retail. Today, there are three models available.

Shatterless rails

Canadian Irwin Cameron Mackie invented the first shatterless rails, which were produced by Nova Scotia's Sydney Steel in July 1931. The new rails, which solved a significant problem of rails cracking under heavy weights, were first used exclusively on the Canadian National Railway.

Electric railway

John Wright is credited with building the first electric railway in Canada. In 1883, an engine owned by Wright was used in an electric railway demonstration by the Toronto Industrial Exhibition at the Canadian National Exhibition, but it proved unable to move any cars. The following year, however, a similar demonstration using a motorized Grand Truck flatcar worked.

Hydrofoil

Better known for his invention of the telephone, Alexander Graham Bell is also the co-inventor of the first successful hydrofoil, the wing-like device that lifts a boat above the water to reduce drag from the hull. Along with his wife Mabel and engineer F.W. Casey Baldwin, Bell began to create the machine he called a "hydrodrome" in 1908 in Baddeck, Nova Scotia. The first hydrofoil (the HD-1), unveiled in 1911, was capable of speeds of up to 72 km per hour.

Most popular sailboat

It figures that the country with the longest shoreline in the world would invent a sailboat that's the world's most popular. In 1969, Bruce Kirby and Ian Bruce invented the Laser, a race-worthy vessel that could be carried on top of a car. They subsequently varied the size of sails to accommodate racers of various skills, and introduced two other versions of the boat, the Radial and the 4.7. Today these vessels are popular with Olympic-calibre sailors around the world.

First hexagonal wind tunnel

Blow me down! The Windee Dome at Western University in London, Ont., is the world's first hexagonal wind tunnel. The unique structure, which boasts a 25 m diameter inner dome and a 40 m diameter outer dome, allows scientists to recreate real wind systems at a large scale under controlled conditions. Opened in 2013, the facility will test models of wind farms and transmission lines and the dispersion of pollutants.

Methyl methacrylate method

He didn't invent it, but while he was a PhD student at Montreal's McGill University in 1931, William Chalmers devised a new method for creating methyl methacrylate, a previously difficult-to-find ingredient necessary to create Plexiglass. Chalmers sold his patent for the process to Britain's Imperial Chemical Industries, who could then mass-produce the product.

Wind tunnel

Aeronautical engineer Wallace Turnbull, born in Saint John, built Canada's first wind tunnel in Rothesay, New Brunswick, in 1902. He worked at the tunnel, his personal laboratory, for the rest of his life, and collaborated with other aviation pioneers, including Alexander Graham Bell.

Variable-pitch propeller

Turnbull (see Wind tunnel, left) is perhaps best known for inventing the variable-pitch propeller, which was first tested in flight in 1927. This propeller, which adjusts the angle at which its blades cut the air, became an aircraft standard that was safe and efficient at all engine speeds. Turnbull licensed the production of the invention and it was perfected by others.

Automatic landing system

Electronics engineer Eric William Leaver, who grew up in Saskatchewan, invented an inertial guidance system (automatic landing system) for aircraft in the 1930s. Subsequent products based on his invention are used all over the world today.

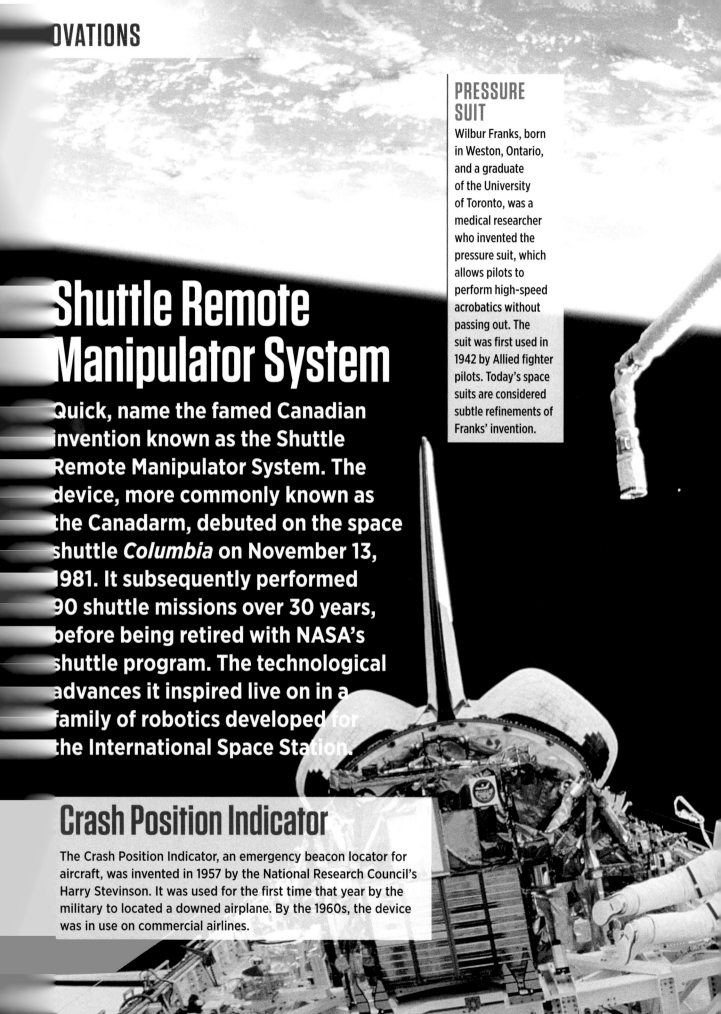

PRESSURE SUIT

Wilbur Franks, born in Weston, Ontario, and a graduate of the University of Toronto, was a medical researcher who invented the pressure suit, which allows pilots to perform high-speed acrobatics without passing out. The suit was first used in 1942 by Allied fighter pilots. Today's space suits are considered subtle refinements of Franks' invention.

Shuttle Remote Manipulator System

Quick, name the famed Canadian invention known as the Shuttle Remote Manipulator System. The device, more commonly known as the Canadarm, debuted on the space shuttle *Columbia* on November 13, 1981. It subsequently performed 90 shuttle missions over 30 years, before being retired with NASA's shuttle program. The technological advances it inspired live on in a family of robotics developed for the International Space Station.

Crash Position Indicator

The Crash Position Indicator, an emergency beacon locator for aircraft, was invented in 1957 by the National Research Council's Harry Stevinson. It was used for the first time that year by the military to located a downed airplane. By the 1960s, the device was in use on commercial airlines.

HUMAN CENTRIFUGE

Franks was responsible for the construction of the nation's first human centrifuge (also the first in Allied nations), which was built for the pressure-suit project in 1941. The lab in Toronto, which was used to test the suit and train jet pilots to withstand g-forces, eventually became the RCAF Institute of Aviation Medicine.

Avro Arrow

It's been called Canada's greatest aeronautical achievement. The Avro Arrow, or CF-105 jet fighter, was the only supersonic jet the country produced. It is said to have been faster (it had a maximum speed of 2,453 km per hour) and more advanced than any other comparable aircraft. Rising costs of production combined with the development of long-range missiles caused the government to cancel the aircraft (on February 20, 1959, a day known as "Black Friday" by some as a result), and all the existing jets were destroyed, along with all related plans and equipment.

EXPLOSIVE VAPOUR DETECTOR

While working at the National Research Council in the 1980s, chemist Lorne Elias developed the portable Explosive Vapour Detector, a device capable of sniffing out hidden bombs. In 1984, the RCMP used a prototype of the device during a visit by the Pope. When security officials were checking the Pope's baggage, a detector went off— triggered by a revolver one of the pontiff's bodyguards had packed in his luggage.

IMAX

IMAX, a movie format that can record and display motion pictures at a far greater size and resolution than traditional film systems, was developed by a group of Canadian filmmakers and unveiled at the Fuji Pavilion at EXPO '70 in Osaka, Japan. The first IMAX projection system debuted at Toronto's Ontario Place in 1971. The world's first IMAX 3D system was revealed at Vancouver's EXPO '86. There are now more than 728 IMAX theatres in 53 countries.

Alkaline battery

You'll get a charge out of this one. Canadian Lewis Urry invented the alkaline battery in 1959. About 80 percent of dry cell batteries in use in the world are based on Urry's invention.

Trivial Pursuit

How else to address this than with a question: Where was the popular game Trivial Pursuit invented? In Montreal, when journalists Chris Haney and Scott Abbott came up with the idea on December 15, 1979.

Instant replay

Did you see that? Now you did, thanks to the invention of instant replay by the CBC in 1955. The technique was first used (where else?) on a broadcast of *Hockey Night in Canada*.

Java

Here's an invention to make you sit up and take notice. Java, the programming language at the root of virtually every networked application, was invented by Canadian James A. Gosling. Sun Microsystems released the first version of Java in 1995.

Electronic organ

A Canadian pioneer of electronic music? Frank Morse Robb invented the first electronic organ in Belleville, Ontario. His Robb Wave Organ didn't hit the market until 1936, although news of his creation had been covered in the *Toronto Star* as early as 1927. Designed to reproduce the sounds of a cathedral pipe organ and considered to sound better than the competing Hammond Organ, the device didn't last long. Its higher price led to its demise by 1941.

Voltage-controlled synthesizer

Electronic music owes a lot, if not its entire existence, to Canadian Hugh Le Caine. In 1945, while working for the National Research Council in Ottawa, Le Caine spent his spare time working on the development of electronic musical instruments, including the Electronic Sackbut, which is considered the first voltage-controlled synthesizer. He went on to create voltage-control systems for a range of uses.

Electronic heart pacemaker

The electronic heart pacemaker was invented in 1949 by Dr. Wilfred Bigelow and Dr. John Callaghan of Toronto, with the help of electrical engineer John Hopps of the National Research Council in Ottawa. In 1958, Arne Larsson was the first person to have an implantable pacemaker. It lasted just three hours. During his lifetime, Larsson had 28 pacemakers before he died at the age of 86.

Electron microscope

Physicist Eli Franklin Burton, born in Green River, Ontario, built the first electron microscope in North America in the late 1930s, with the assistance of Cecil Hall, James Hillier and A.F. Prebus.

Cobalt bomb

Medical physicist Dr. Harold Johns and his graduate students at the University of Saskatchewan were the first researchers to successfully treat a cancer patient using cobalt-60 radiation therapy, in 1951. The technology, also known as the "cobalt bomb," significantly changed cancer treatment and saved and prolonged the lives of millions of cancer patients.

Mobile blood transfusion

Norman Bethune, born in Gravenhurst, Ontario, in 1890, devised the world's first mobile blood transfusion service during the early days of the Spanish War, which began in 1936. Blood was collected in cities and transported to the front lines. The service is considered the greatest innovation in military medicine to arise from that war.

Mobile operating theatre

Bethune also created the globe's first mobile operating theatre, in 1938 while working for the Chinese Communist Party during the Second Sino-Japanese War. The facility, which could be carried by two donkeys, was put to good use. Bethune is reported to have operated on 115 soldiers during a 69-hour period without pause under heavy artillery fire.

Bethune rib shears

Bethune is also known for a number of medical innovations earlier in his career, while working near Montreal in the late 1920s and 1930s. Bethune pioneered numerous new medical techniques and instruments, one of which — the Bethune rib shears — is still manufactured.

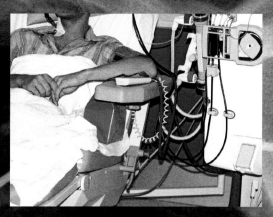

Artificial kidney

In the 1940s, Dr. Gordon Murray of Toronto independently designed the first artificial kidney in North America, unaware that doctors in Europe were working on a similar invention. It was tested extensively on animals, but after trials on four patients at Toronto General Hospital, his project was abandoned. Dr. Murray's contributions to medicine didn't stop there, however: he was also the first to transplant a human heart valve.

Electric wheelchair

Born in Hamilton, Ontario, George Klein invented the electric wheelchair in 1955 while working for the National Research Council. Originally created for disabled military personnel, the first prototype of the joystick-controlled, battery-operated wheelchair was presented to the United States Veterans Administration.

WEEVAC 6

Here's proof big things can come in small packages. The WEEVAC 6, the world's first evacuation stretcher designed for infants, was created in 1987 by Canadian Wendy Murphy.

T-cell receptor

This could get complicated, so let's keep things simple. In 1984, Canadian Dr. Tak Wah Mak co-discovered the T-cell receptor. This led doctors to a better understanding of how the immune system recognizes and fights infections, allowing them to create new, more effective drugs. The discovery is considered the Holy Grail of immunology.

Aerial survey

In 1920, the first experimental aerial survey was taken over Ottawa. The technique became a revolutionary topographical survey method and was eventually used to survey and create an inventory of Canadian forests from the air. Because of the initiative, Canada has one of the world's most extensive collections of aerial photography.

WonderBra

It's a name synonymous with lady's undergarments: WonderBra. And in 1939, the Canadian Lady Corset Company was the first to begin marketing bras under that brand name.

Strapless bra

The WonderBra brand had more firsts in women's underwear. The brand introduced the first strapless bra, the Winkie, in the 1940s. It also developed the diagonal shoulder strap in the same decade.

FIRST BRA ADS ON TELEVISION

In 1972, WonderBra ran the first television ads in North America to feature a model wearing a bra. Before that, women's underwear had been displayed on mannequins or bust forms.

Standard time

Imagine having to wear six watches to keep track of what time it is in different places. That's exactly what some people did before Canadian engineer Sandford Fleming devised the concept of Universal Standard Time in 1879. UST divides the world into 24 times zones. In each zone clocks indicate the same time, with one-hour difference between adjoining zones. At first, governments and the scientific community dismissed the idea, but eventually UST was accepted and went into effect on January 1, 1885.

Heli-skiing

Heli-skiing, in which a helicopter takes skiers to far-flung mountain runs, was invented in Canada in 1965. Hans Gmoser, who'd come to Canada from Austria in 1951, pioneered the concept in British Columbia's Bugaboo Mountians, where he built a lodge that still operates as a heli-skiing operation today.

Beauty products

Shhh. Here's a uniquely Canadian beauty secret: Elizabeth Arden, the international beauty company, was founded by a Canadian. Born in Woodbridge, Ontario, on December 31, 1884, Florence Nightingale Graham (who changed her name to Elizabeth Arden) opened a beauty salon on New York City's Fifth Avenue in 1910. She is known for a number of firsts in the beauty industry, including creating the first travel-size beauty products.

Geographic Information System

Canadian geographer Roger Tomlinson is known as the "Father of GIS" for his role in developing the first Geographic Information System. GIS, developed in the 1960s, is a program that combines spatial analysis and digital mapping to process large quantities of data. Essentially, GIS combines cartography, statistical analysis and databases.

Canadian Eskimo dog

This is one old dog. The Canadian Eskimo Dog is considered the oldest indigenous dog species still in existence. The breed, often used to pull sleds, is believed to have originated around 1100 to 1200 AD in what is now the Canadian Arctic. The breed, also known as the Canadian Inuit Dog, is the official animal of Nunavut.

Nova Scotia duck tolling retriever

The Nova Scotia duck tolling retriever, the official dog of Nova Scotia, was the first Canadian dog breed to be named a provincial symbol. Developed in the early 19th century, the species was breed to lure (or toll) and retrieve waterfowl.

Newfoundland dog

The Newfoundland dog is another made-in-Canada dog species. Little is known of the breed's exact origins, though the species was first named in the late 17th century. Nearly as at home in the water — if not more so — than the land, the Newfoundland was originally used as a ship dog (to carry lines to shore or for water rescues).

Tahltan bear dog

Though it's now believed to be extinct, the Tahltan bear dog is the last of the five Canadian dog species recognized by the Canadian Kennel Club. The breed was used by the Tahltan Indians of northeastern British Columbia to hunt bear and lynx. Only nine were ever registered with the CKC after the breed was recognized in 1940.

Labrador retriever

The Labrador retriever, which originated on the island of Newfoundland, was first recognized as a breed by England's Kennel Club in 1903, though records describing the breed date from as early as the mid-18th century. Known as a "water dog," Labs were appreciated for their intelligence and outgoing nature.

First train

Trains are an important part of the foundation of our nation, and Canada's first railway was opened in 1836 between La Prairie and Saint-Jean-sur-Richelieu, Quebec. It was called the "Champlain and St. Lawrence Railroad," since it connected the St. Lawrence River to Lake Champlain. Prior to the railway's official opening, test runs of the locomotive were conducted at night so as not to frighten locals.

Molson railway

The final legacy of John Molson was his key role in the construction of Canada's first railway, which was just starting when he died in 1836. Molson financed the Champlain and Saint Lawrence Railroad (see First train, left), which ran between La Prairie and Saint-Jean-sur-Richelieu.

First trans-continental railway

The nation's first transcontinental railway, the Canadian Pacific Railway, was completed on November 7, 1885. The last spike was driven in at Craigellachie, British Columbia.

Longest railway tunnel

Yes, there is a light at the end of the tunnel. Canada is home to the longest railway tunnel in North America, the 14.7 km Mount MacDonald Tunnel in British Columbia's Selkirk Mountains. Construction of the tunnel was completed in 1988.

First trans-continental train

On June 28, 1886, the country's first transcontinental train left Montreal for Port Moody, British Columbia. It arrived on July 4.

First trans-border railway

The Grand Trunk Railway, incorporated in 1852, was the first trans-border railway in North America. It ran from Sarnia, Ontario, to Portland, Maine. Trains began running from Montreal to Portland on the route in 1853.

FIRST SUBMARINE TUNNEL

The world's first international submarine tunnel, linking Sarnia, Ontario, with Port Huron, Michigan, opened on September 19, 1891. The St. Clair Tunnel, almost 2 km long, was used by the Grand Trunk Railroad.

First trains with Wi-Fi

Canada's VIA Rail was the first railway company in North America to make Wi-Fi service available to passengers, in 2006.

Oldest sternwheeler

The SS *Moyie* is the world's oldest intact passenger sternwheeler. The ship was retired in 1957 after 59 years of service for the Canadian Pacific Railway's BC Lake and River Service. The Moyie performed a number of duties over its lifetime and was the last operating sternwheeler in Canada. The ship is a national historic site today at its home in Kaslo, British Columbia.

Free ferry

Looking for a free ride? Try British Columbia's Kootenay Lake Ferry, the world's longest free ferry ride. There are actually two ferries that run year-round between Kootenay Bay and Balfour, a 35-minute trip. Both vessels — the *Osprey 2000* and the *MV Balfour* — accommodate vehicles of all sizes, including RVs.

First Canadian steamboat

John Molson, founder of the Molson brewery, was responsible for the construction of the first entirely Canadian-made steamboat in 1809. Molson eventually extended the endeavour to a fleet of 22 ships. The venture helped open the St. Lawrence and Canada to trade and settlement.

Oldest ferry

Halifax is home to the continent's oldest, continuous-running saltwater ferry service, which began in 1752. Known as the "Dartmouth ferry" at the time, the service connected the vast farmland on the Dartmouth side of Halifax Harbour with Halifax, providing the city with fresh food. The original ferry was a rowboat with a sail.

First steam ship across the Atlantic

The HMS *Royal William* was the first Canadian ship to cross the Atlantic completely under steam power. It was first launched in Quebec on April 27, 1831. Later that year, the ship made several voyages between Quebec and Atlantic Canada, but in 1932 it was quarantined because of a cholera epidemic. On August 18, 1833, with seven passengers and a load of coal, it started the 25-day journey from Pictou, Nova Scotia to Gravesend, England. The ship was eventually sold to the Spanish Navy.

Largest grain capacity

Ontario's Port of Thunder Bay has the largest grain storage capacity in North America. The port's eight terminals have a capacity of 1.2 million tonnes.

BUSIEST PORT

Port Metro, Vancouver is the nation's largest and busiest port. More than 70 million tonnes of cargo, delivered from more than 3,000 different container ships, pass through the port each year.

Northwest passage west to east

The RCMP auxiliary schooner *St. Roch* holds a special place (or two or three!) in Canadian maritime history. Designed to avoid being crushed by ice, the wooden, sail-powered *St. Roch* was the first ship to sail the Northwest Passage from west to east in 1940–42 The ship was trapped in the ice for two seasons, before it completed its journey on October 11, 1942.

CIRCUM-NAVIGATING NORTH AMERICA

To complete its maritime milestones, the *St. Roch* also became the first ship to circumnavigate North America, in 1950.

First solo voyage around the world

Joshua Slocum, a native of Annapolis County, Nova Scotia, became the first person to sail solo around the world. He departed from Boston on April 24, 1895, in his ship the *Spray* on the 74,000 km voyage, which took three years to complete. His book on the journey, *Sailing Alone around the World*, has been continuously in print since it was published in 1900.

First through the Northwest Passage

Canada's Northwest Passage has long transfixed explorers searching for a navigable route across the top of North America. In 1853–54, British explorer Robert McClure was the first recorded person to complete the route, partly by sledge, from west to east.

Northwest Passage both ways

Thanks to its two voyages through the Northwest Passage in 1940–1942 and 1944, the *St. Roch* became the first ship to sail the legendary route in both directions.

NORTHWEST PASSAGE EAST TO WEST

Norwegian explorer Roald Amundsen was the first person to navigate Canada's Northwest Passage by ship, from 1903–1906. Amundsen sailed his ship *Gjoa* west and south of Lancaster Sound through Peel Sound and through Queen Maud and Coronation gulfs in the western Arctic.

NORTHWEST PASSAGE WEST TO EAST IN ONE SEASON

The HMCS *Labrador*, an icebreaker of the Royal Canadian Navy, was the first vessel to travel the Northwest Passage west to east in a single season, in 1954.

NORTHWEST PASSAGE EAST TO WEST IN ONE SEASON

The *St. Roch* was the first vessel to travel the Northwest Passage in one season, which it did, east to west, in 1944, between July 22 and October 16. It travelled a "new" route, sailing through Lancaster Sound, through Prince of Wales Strait and along the northern Alaska coast.

First to sink U-boat

On September 10, 1941, the *Chambly* and the *Moose Jaw* were the first Canadian warships to sink a U-boat. In a coordinated attack, the *Chambly* heavily damaged the German sub U-501 with five depth charges. The sub's captain opened its hatches when it surfaced, and it quickly sank, killing 11 Germans and one Canadian member of a boarding party.

First Naval dockyard

Built in 1759, the Naval Dockyard in Halifax was the first naval dockyard in North America.

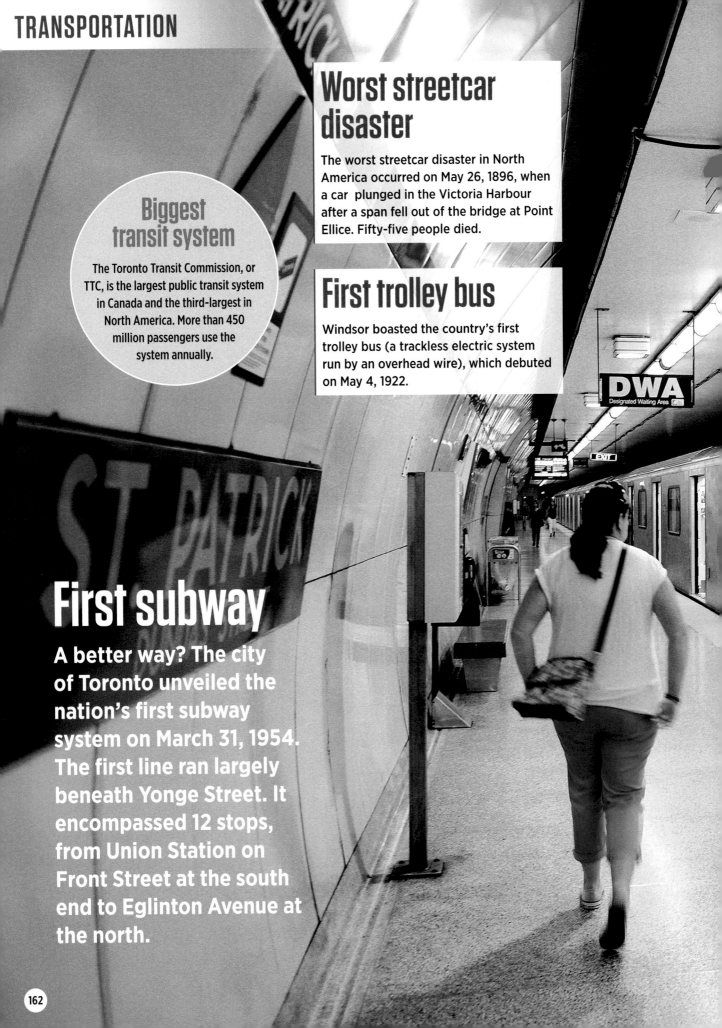

Worst streetcar disaster

The worst streetcar disaster in North America occurred on May 26, 1896, when a car plunged in the Victoria Harbour after a span fell out of the bridge at Point Ellice. Fifty-five people died.

Biggest transit system

The Toronto Transit Commission, or TTC, is the largest public transit system in Canada and the third-largest in North America. More than 450 million passengers use the system annually.

First trolley bus

Windsor boasted the country's first trolley bus (a trackless electric system run by an overhead wire), which debuted on May 4, 1922.

First subway

A better way? The city of Toronto unveiled the nation's first subway system on March 31, 1954. The first line ran largely beneath Yonge Street. It encompassed 12 stops, from Union Station on Front Street at the south end to Eglinton Avenue at the north.

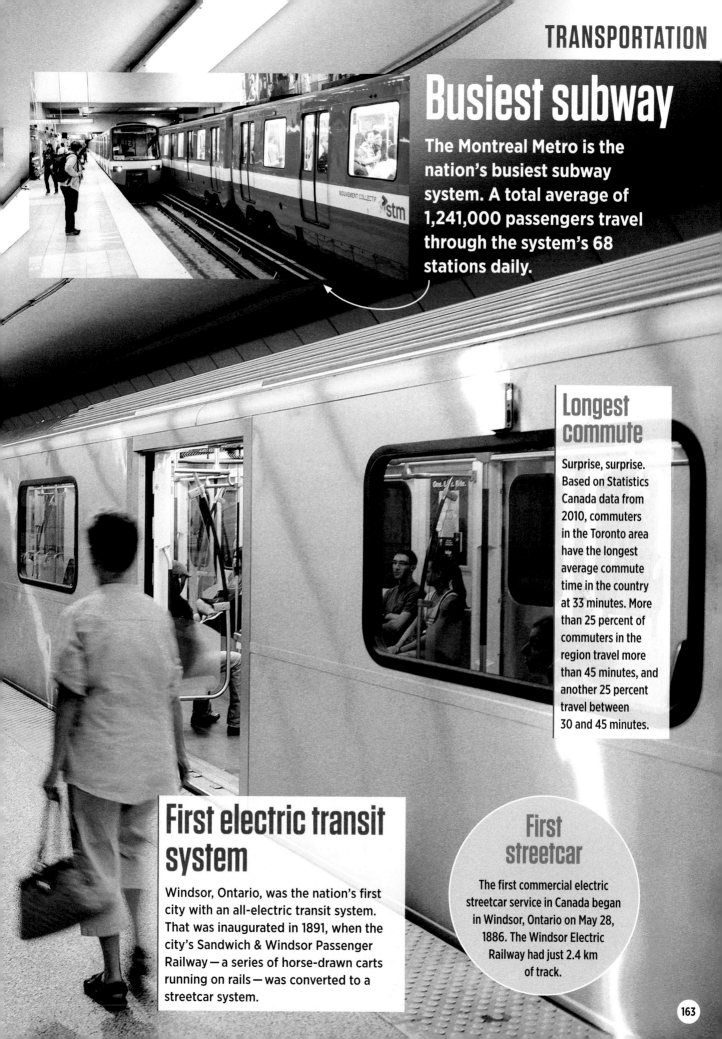

Busiest subway

The Montreal Metro is the nation's busiest subway system. A total average of 1,241,000 passengers travel through the system's 68 stations daily.

Longest commute

Surprise, surprise. Based on Statistics Canada data from 2010, commuters in the Toronto area have the longest average commute time in the country at 33 minutes. More than 25 percent of commuters in the region travel more than 45 minutes, and another 25 percent travel between 30 and 45 minutes.

First electric transit system

Windsor, Ontario, was the nation's first city with an all-electric transit system. That was inaugurated in 1891, when the city's Sandwich & Windsor Passenger Railway — a series of horse-drawn carts running on rails — was converted to a streetcar system.

First streetcar

The first commercial electric streetcar service in Canada began in Windsor, Ontario on May 28, 1886. The Windsor Electric Railway had just 2.4 km of track.

First car

The first car manufactured in Canada was the Taylor Steam Buggy, built by Henry Seth Taylor of Stanstead, Quebec, in 1867. The car was powered by a coil-fired boiler at the back and used a handle to control its speed and a horizontal bar to steer.

First electric car

The buzz these days over electric cars seems a little funny when you consider the nation's first electric car was built more than 100 years ago, in 1893. Using a battery and motor designed by William Still, Frederick B. Featherstonehaugh commissioned the Dixon Carriage Works to build it. The two-person car was capable of about 25 km per hour.

First car in production

The nation's first gasoline-powered car to be put into production was the LeRoy, which debuted in 1902. Fewer than 20 of the cars were produced by the LeRoy Manufacturing Co. of Berlin, Ontario (now Kitchener), before the company closed in 1904. The cost of a brand-new LeRoy in 1903? A mere $650 (the average annual income at the time was about $275).

The most horse-drawn vehicles

The continent's largest collection of horse-drawn vehicles resides at the Remington Carriage Museum in Cardston, Alberta. The museum boasts more than 270 carriages, buggies, wagons and sleighs from the 19th and early 20th centuries.

Most road

If someone tells you to hit the road in Saskatchewan, be prepared for a very long walk. The province has more road surface than any other in the country: a total of 250,000 km.

First gas car

The first successful gasoline-powered car in Canada was built by George Foote Foss in Sherbrooke, Quebec, in 1896.

No cars allowed

Can you imagine banning cars? Prince Edward Island did it in 1908. The government instituted the prohibition because many islanders thought the automobile was too noisy and scared horses. In 1913, the restriction was reduced and driving was banned on Tuesdays, Fridays, Saturdays and Sundays. It wasn't until 1918 that the province rescinded the ban entirely.

More people take cars

According to 2010 data from Statistics Canada, 82 percent of Canadians commute to work by car (12 percent take public transit, while 6 percent walk or cycle).

First cross-Canada car trip

Are we there yet? The first cross-Canada car trip took 49 days. Writer Tom Wilby and driver/mechanic Jack Haney left Halifax on August 27, 1912, in an REO The Fifth (the fifth car designed by Ransom E. Olds), and arrived in Vancouver on October 14. During the journey, the duo travelled 298 km on their best day and just 19 on their worst.

First gas station

Here's a fill 'er up first: the nation's first gas station opened in Vancouver in June 1907. Prior to the development of specialized gas stations, drivers had to fill up at distribution sites, which were typically located on the edges of towns or cities.

LOWEST ROAD

The lowest point on a public road in Canada is in the George Massey Tunnel under the Fraser River near Vancouver International Airport (it's 20 m below sea level). The 629 m tunnel, which opened in 1959, was considered an engineering marvel. It was the first project in North America to use immersed-tube technology. Six concrete segments, each 105 m long and weighing 16,783 tonnes, were built on dry land, joined, sealed and sunk into place.

First international tunnel

The Detroit-Windsor Tunnel, which links the two cities in Michigan and Ontario, respectively, was the world's first international vehicular tunnel. The 1,573 m tunnel opened on November 3, 1930, after more than a year of construction and a cost of $23 million.

Snow road

Winter driving here is recommended. The Wapusk Trail road is the longest seasonal winter road in the world, according to Guinness World Records. The 752 km road is constructed annually in January between Gillam, Manitoba, and Peawanuk, Ontario, on snow and ice.

THE QUEEN'S HIGHWAY

The Queen Elizabeth Way, a highway from Toronto to Fort Erie, Ontario, was the nation's first four-lane, controlled-access highway. The highway was officially opened by Queen Elizabeth (who later became the Queen Mother) at St. Catharines, Ontario, on June 7, 1939. At the time, the roadway was the longest multi-lane, divided highway in the Commonwealth.

Arctic Circle highway

Opened on August 18, 1979, the Dempster Highway was Canada's first all-weather road to cross the Arctic Circle. The Dempster runs some 720 km from Dawson, Yukon, to Inuvik, Northwest Territories.

Fastest highway

The Alaska Highway, which runs from Dawson Creek, British Columbia, to Fairbanks, Alaska, was built faster than any other highway in the world. The entire 2,451 km freeway was built in less than a year, through 1942 and 1943.

Biggest dump truck

In Sparwood, British Columbia, they call it simply "The Truck." The truck in question, a 1974 Terex Titan, is the largest tandem axel dump truck in the world. The 350-tonne, 20-m-long, 3,300-hp vehicle is so big, it can fit two Greyhound buses and two pickups in the box at the same time.

Fly or swim

There are no communities in Nunavut that are accessible by road or rail. Everything arrives by air or sea.

Third-longest highway

The Trans-Canada Highway, which runs 7,821 km from St. John's to Victoria, is the one of the world's longest highways, along with the Trans-Siberian Highway and Australia's Highway 1. When the road opened at B.C.'s Rogers Pass on July 30, 1962, more than 3,000 km of it remained unpaved. Eventually completed in 1970, the Trans-Canada cost a total of $1 billion dollars to build.

Busiest highway

If you regularly drive along Highway 401 through Toronto, this may come as little surprise — and may be dismally deflating: the stretch is the busiest highway on the continent. It's estimated that an average of more than 425,000 vehicles travel the route daily, and some days the traffic surpasses half a million vehicles.

Fuel-cell factory

The Mercedes-Benz plant in Burnaby, British Columbia, is the planet's first automated facility dedicated to producing automotive fuel cells. It opened in June 2012.

First fuel-cell car

The world's first fuel-cell car, Daimler-Benz's NECar I, used fuel-cell technology created by British Columbia's Ballard Power Systems. Invented in 1994, the car required 12 fuel-cell stacks to create 50 kW of power.

First traffic lights

The first traffic lights in Canada went up on June 11, 1925, at the intersection of Main and King streets in east Hamilton. The traffic light, which was made in the United States, proved problematic, as it had been designed for use at right-angle intersections, while Main and King crisscross at an angle. As a result, drivers were sometimes confused as to which light was meant for them. Another problem? Local residents weren't fond of the loud bell that accompanied the amber light.

The most manuals

Here's a unique niche achievement. The Reynolds-Alberta Museum, just west of Wetaskiwin, Alberta, is home to the nation's largest collection of publically held service and operation manuals for cars, trucks and planes. The museum's resource centre houses hundreds of parts books, sales catalogues and brochures, magazines and other reference files. The museum is also home to the nation's second-largest collection of vintage aircraft (after the Canadian Aviation and Space Museum in Ottawa).

MEA (Membrane Electrode Assembly)

FRONT ST. W

Fuel-cell bus

The world's largest fleet of fuel-cell buses were part of BC Transit's fleet at the Vancouver 2010 Winter Olympics. The 20 buses (still operating in Whistler and representing 87 percent of that city's fleet), have a top speed of 90 km per hour and are estimated to stay in service for 20 years.

First fuel-cell bus

British Columbia-based Ballard Power Systems unveiled the world's first fuel-cell bus in 1993. The 9.75 m shuttle bus could carry 20 people, and created less greenhouse gas emissions than conventional buses.

First computerized traffic control

Toronto was the first city in the world with a computerized traffic control system. In 1963, the city implemented the system to automate traffic signals. It required a 4.5-tonne air conditioning unit to keep it cool. Essentially, it was a clock that used predetermined plans to regulate traffic patterns during different parts of the day.

First Canadian flight

The first flight in Canada occurred in Baddeck, Nova Scotia, on February 23, 1909. The silver-winged biplane, called the "Silver Dart," was piloted by J.A.D. McCurdy. It flew 800 m at an average speed of 65 km per hour. The Silver Dart flew 200 flights before it was damaged beyond repair.

Seventh pilot

He wasn't the first, but he was darn close. Frederick Baldwin "Casey" Walker became the seventh person to pilot a plane (and the first Canadian and Commonwealth subject to do so). On March 12, 1908, at Hammondsport, New York he flew a plane called the "Red Wing," a biplane with the propeller located behind the wing. It flew a distance of 97.2 m before flipping to its side and crashing.

First metal bush plane

The de Havilland DHC-2 Beaver was the first all-metal bush plane designed and built in Canada. It was particularly well-known for its ability on short takeoffs and landings. More Beavers were built than any other Canadian aircraft to date: 1,692 between 1947 and 1968.

First bush plane

The bush plane is synonymous with Canada's hinterland. The first successful, all-Canadian bush plane was the Noorduyn Norseman, which first flew in November 1935. More than 900 were built in Montreal by its designer, R.B.C. Noorduyn. The aircraft's large cabin and its ability to take off and land in tight spots made the plane a common workhorse of the nation's north.

Firsts in aviation

J.A.D. McCurdy was a man of many firsts. Some highlights:

- He co-founded the first aircraft manufacturing company in Canada, The Canadian Aerodrome Company, in April 1909.
- He performed the first figure-eight manoeuvre in an airplane in the world on August 28, 1908.
- He was the first Canadian to be issued a pilot's licence.
- He established the first aviation school in Canada.
- He was the first to fly a "flying boat," on May 1, 1910.
- At the time of his death, June 25, 1961, when he was 75, he was the world's oldest pilot.

First airplane

The Baddeck No. 1 was the first made-in-Canada powered aircraft. Built by the Canadian Aerodrome Company its first flight was on August 12, 1909.

First bush pilot

Bush flying was hugely important to the early days of exploring Canada's vast hinterland. It started out as a means to spot forest fires. Stuart Graham was the first to fly such patrols over Quebec's St. Maurice River Valley in 1919, in two war-surplus Curtiss HS-2L flying boats. Thus began a key method of accessing the country's more remote regions.

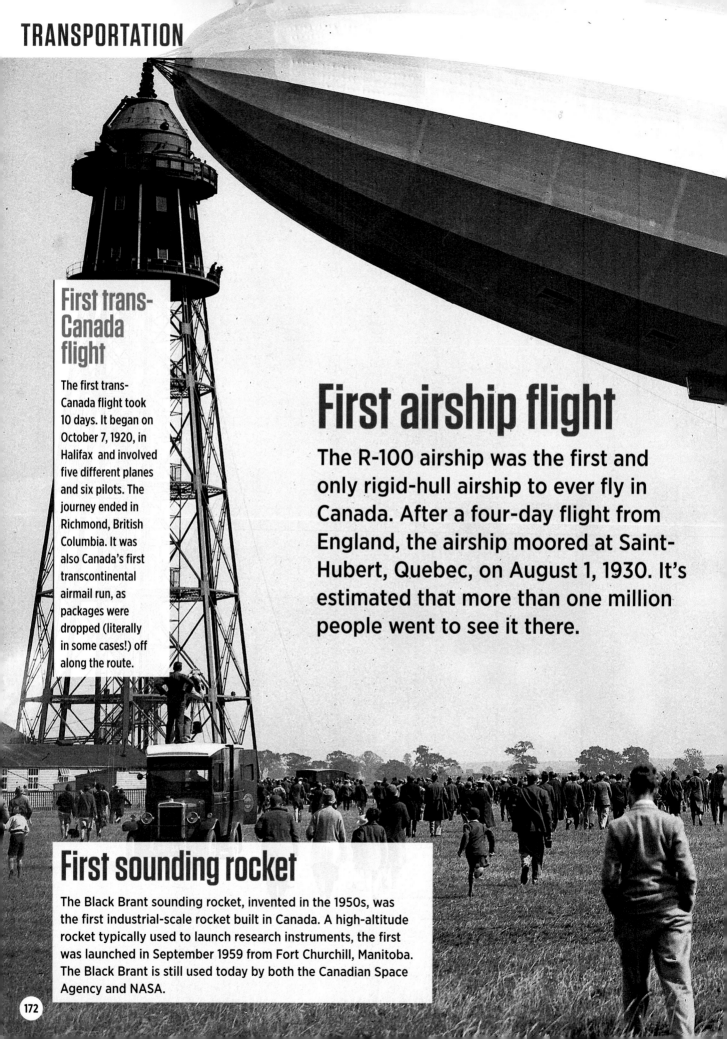

First trans-Canada flight

The first trans-Canada flight took 10 days. It began on October 7, 1920, in Halifax and involved five different planes and six pilots. The journey ended in Richmond, British Columbia. It was also Canada's first transcontinental airmail run, as packages were dropped (literally in some cases!) off along the route.

First airship flight

The R-100 airship was the first and only rigid-hull airship to ever fly in Canada. After a four-day flight from England, the airship moored at Saint-Hubert, Quebec, on August 1, 1930. It's estimated that more than one million people went to see it there.

First sounding rocket

The Black Brant sounding rocket, invented in the 1950s, was the first industrial-scale rocket built in Canada. A high-altitude rocket typically used to launch research instruments, the first was launched in September 1959 from Fort Churchill, Manitoba. The Black Brant is still used today by both the Canadian Space Agency and NASA.

First non-stop trans-Canada flight

On January 14, 1949, the first non-stop trans-Canada flight, from Vancouver to Halifax, took place. A Canadair North Star airplane took eight and a half hours to make the flight.

First flight over Rockies

The first flight over the Canadian Rocky Mountains occurred on August 7, 1919. Pilot Ernest Hoy flew a Curtiss JN-4 from Vancouver to Calgary. The flight took 16.5 hours.

First water bomber

It figures that the only plane in the world built specifically to fight forest fires would be Canadian. The Canadair CL-215 was the world's first amphibious water bomber. Its first flight was October 23, 1967. The plane features two 2,271-litre tanks, which take 8 to 10 seconds to scoop water and just 2 seconds to dump.

First forest fire spotted from the air

Fire! On July 7, 1919, Stuart Graham and W. Kahre become the first to spot a forest fire in Canada from the air, while they were flying over Quebec's St. Maurice River.

First landing pad for UFOs

Who needs Area 51? Canada has the world's first UFO landing pad. The unique landmark was built in the town of St. Paul, Alberta, and opened on June 3, 1967. In 1996, a UFO interpretive centre was built to accompany the pad.

Biggest airport

Toronto's Pearson International Airport is Canada's largest and busiest airport, and as a result, the country's primary air hub. It handles more than 30 percent of the nation's air travel. In 2012, it saw more than 400,000 flights and nearly 35 million passengers pass through. Pearson is the second-busiest gateway to Europe and handles the most United States–Canada air traffic.

Worst Canadian air crash

The year 1985 was a particularly bad year for Canadian air disasters. The worst airline incident associated with Canada, and the third worst in the world, occurred on June 23, when Air India flight 182 from Toronto crashed into the north Atlantic off the coast of Ireland. It's suspected a terrorist bomb caused the disaster, which killed all 329 passengers, including 280 Canadians.

Worst air crash in Canada

The worst air crash in Canadian history occurred December 12, 1985, when an Arrow Airlines DC-8 enroute to Kentucky crashed just after takeoff, after refuelling at Gander, Newfoundland. All 256 passengers, including 248 members of the United States 101st Airborne Division, were killed.

AVIATION LICENCE FIRSTS

Roland J. Groome was a man of firsts. Along with Edward Clarke and Bob McCombie, Groome formed the Aerial Service Company in 1919 and built the first licensed aerodrome in Canada in Regina. Groome would become the first licensed commercial aviator in the nation. One of the company's aircraft became the country's first licensed commercial airplane: the JN-4 Canuck was registration number G-CAAA.

First aviation meet

On June 25, 1910, Canada's first aviation meet (and the largest in North America at the time) took flight. The Montreal Aviation Meet boasted 10 airplanes and 9 pilots.

First intercity flight

The first intercity flight in Canada took place in 1911, when famed pilot J.A.D McCurdy won an airplane race from Hamilton to Toronto — after giving his competitors a 10-minute head start.

Longest runway

Slated to open in June, 2014, the new fourth runway at Calgary International Airport will become Canada's longest, at 4,267 m long and 61 m wide. It was planned as part of the airport's $2 billion development program, in response to passenger volume doubling in the last two decades. The new landing strip will be capable of landing the world's largest aircraft, the A380 and B747-800. One million square m of concrete will be used to pave the new runway and related taxiways, and more than 5,000 LED lights with illuminate the area.

First jetliner

The Avro Canada C102 Jetliner was a first in many respects. Built by Avro Canada in 1949, it was the first Canadian jet to fly and the first commercial jet in North America (and the second in the world: just two weeks behind the first!). The prototype jet's first flight was over Toronto's Malton Airport on August 10, 1949. The following year, the plane was the first to make an airmail delivery by jet on April 18, 1950, on a flight from Toronto to New York.

First stars in cement

Early Hollywood actress Mary Pickford, and her husband at the time, Douglas Fairbanks, were the first stars to cast their hands and feet in cement in front of the Grauman's Chinese Theatre in Hollywood, on April 30, 1927. Known as "America's sweetheart," Pickford was born in Toronto on April 8, 1892.

The first kiss

When is a kiss not just a kiss? When the year is 1895, and the smooch in question is the first in the very early days of moving pictures. May Irwin, of Whitby, Ontario, a Canadian actress and the most well-loved comedienne of her time, puckered up in the short film *The Kiss*. Many considered the peck a scandal.

Canadian Hollywood sign

It's quite possibly one of the most recognizable signs in the world — indeed, some call it the most famous sign on the planet. But did you know that the Hollywood sign in Los Angeles, California, was built by Canadian Mack Sennett in 1923? Sennett, born in Richmond, Quebec, on January 17, 1880, became a film actor, director and producer, co-founding the Keystone production company and "discovering" a number of early Hollywood stars, including Charlie Chaplin.

Canadian Warner Bros.

How's this for a Canadian connection to Hollywood royalty? Along with his brothers Henry M., Albert and Sam, Jack L. Warner, who was born in London, Ontario, on August 2, 1892, founded Warner Bros. Pictures Inc., the massive Hollywood film studio, in 1923. Jack became one of the most famous and significant film executives of early Hollywood.

First movie star

A Canadian first in Hollywood history: Florence Lawrence, born in Hamilton, Ontario, on January 2, 1886, is believed to be the first movie star known publically by her real name. (Studios didn't use actors' real names for fear they'd demand more money). As part of a publicity stunt for the movie *The Broken Oath* in 1909, her true identity was revealed. Lawrence, who appeared in almost 300 films starting in 1906, is also considered the world's first movie star.

First Canadian movie hit

Considered by many as Canada's first filmmaker, James Freer immigrated to Canada from England in 1888 and settled in Brandon Hills, Manitoba. Freer was sponsored to tour Britain with his films starting in April 1898. His *Ten years in Manitoba — 25,000 instantaneous photos upon a half-a-mile of Edison films*, which depicted scenes of everyday Canadians, was considered a popular and commercial success.

First talkie

Warner Bros. Pictures Inc., co-founded by Canadian Jack L. Warner, released the first movie with synchronized sound, *The Jazz Singer*, in 1927.

First documentary

Nanook of the North, a silent movie from 1922 about a group of Inuit living on the coast of Hudson Bay, is widely regarded as the first full-length documentary film.

First documentary Oscar

Following in that tradition, the National Film Board's *Churchill's Island*, a documentary about the Battle of Britain, won the first Oscar for the category in 1941.

OLDEST OSCAR WINNER

Who says you can't teach an old dog new tricks? Canadian actor Christopher Plummer, born in Toronto on December 12, 1929, is the oldest actor to ever win an Oscar. Plummer captured the 2012 Academy Award for Best Supporting Actor for his role in *Beginners* at the age of 82.

First woman in Royal Society of Canada

Author Gabrielle Roy was the first woman to be admitted to the Royal Society of Canada — a collection of scholars, artists and scientists aiming to promote learning and research — in 1947.

CANADIAN *SATURDAY NIGHT LIVE*

Mad television genius

While the rumours of his being the inspiration for Dr. Evil of Austin Powers fame have been denied, there's no question television producer Lorne Michaels is a mad genius, after a fashion. Born in Toronto on November 17, 1944, Michaels' most noteworthy accomplishment is as the creator and executive producer of *Saturday Night Live*, the longest-running and highest-rated late-night television show ever.

Highest-grossing movies

Talk about Hollywood North! James Cameron, born in Kapuskasing, Ontario, is the writer and director of the two highest-grossing movies of all time, *Avatar* (2009) and *Titanic* (1997). The two films have combined to gross nearly $500 million dollars, with *Avatar* besting *Titanic* at $2,782.3 million to $2,186.8 million, as of early 2013.

Oscars for Canadian siblings

Here's a unique Canadian milestone from the Oscars: brother and sister Douglas and Norma Shearer are the only siblings to ever win Academy Awards in the same year. In 1931, Douglas took the Oscar for Best Sound Recording for *The Big House*, while Norma captured Best Actress for her role in *The Divorcee*.

179

First fiction

Julia Catherine Hart, born on March 10, 1796, in Fredericton, penned the first novel by a Canadian to be published in Canada. Hart's *St. Ursula's Convent*, which explores the dual heritage of French and English cultures in Canada, was published in 1824.

First famous fiction

Thomas Chandler Haliburton, born in Windsor, Nova Scotia, on December 17, 1796, is considered the first Canadian fiction writer to achieve international recognition for his work. It was Haliburton's *The Clockmaker*, also known as *The Sayings and Doings of Sam Slick of Slickville*, published in book form in 1836, which first gained the writer a serious following in the United States and Britian. The book first appeared in 22 installments in the *Novascotian* newspaper.

First best-seller

Beautiful Joe: An Autobiography of a Dog, by Margaret Marshall Saunders, born on April 13, 1861, in Milton, Nova Scotia, is believed to be the first Canadian book to sell one million copies. It was published in 1894.

FIRST CANADIAN *PRIX GONCOURT*

Antonine Maillet, born in Bouctouche, New Brunswick, on May 10, 1929, was the first Canadian, and first non-French citizen, to win the *Prix Goncourt*, one of France's most important literary awards. Maillet won the prize for her 1979 novel, *Pélagie-la-charette*.

King of Kid-Lit

Quick: name the best-selling Canadian author of all time. Did you know it was Canada's "King of Kid-Lit" Robert Munsch? Munsch, who lives in Guelph, Ontario, has penned more than 40 books, with total sales of more than 30 million copies.

Most Governor General awards

Looking for Governor General–approved literature? Look no further than the work of author Hugh MacLennan or Michael Ondaatje. Each has won more Governor General awards for literature than anyone else: a total of five each.

First Governor General awards

The Governor General's Literary Awards were first presented in 1936. The first recipients were Bertram Brooker (fiction), for his book *Think of the Earth*, and T.B. Roberton (non-fiction), for a series of newspaper pieces.

First Canadian *Prix Femina Étranger*

Considered by many to be one of Canada's most important authors, Gabrielle Roy, born in St. Boniface, Manitoba, on March 22, 1909, was the first Canadian author to win the French *Prix Femina Étranger*. Roy captured the French literary award granted to the best novel by a foreigner for her first novel, *Bonheur d'occasion* (*The Tin Flute*) in 1945.

First Booker

Author Michael Ondaatje was the first Canadian to win the Man Booker Prize, a £50,000 literary award for the best novel of the year written by a citizen of the United Kingdom, the Commonwealth or the Republic of Ireland. Ondaatje and his novel *The English Patient* shared the 1992 Booker with Barry Unsworth and his work *Sacred Hunger*.

Superman

Superman, created by Canadian Joe Schuster and American Jerome Siegel, made his first appearance in the June 1938 issue of *Action Comics

Number One hit

Guess who was the first Canadian-based band to have a Number One hit in the United States? The question's the answer. "American Woman" by The Guess Who, based in Winnipeg, Manitoba, hit the top of the Billboard Hot 100 list the weeks of May 9, 16 and 23 in 1970.

First Platinum

Band April Wine, formed in Halifax in 1969, became the first Canadian group to achieve a Platinum album (100,000 sales) in Canada for advance sales: for the record *The Whole World's Goin' Crazy*, released in September 1976.

One million records

Singer-songwriter Bryan Adams, born in Kingston, Ontario, on November 5, 1959, was the first Canadian musician to sell one million albums in Canada, for his 1984 album *Reckless*.

Best-selling American debut

Musician Alanis Morissette, born in Ottawa on June 1, 1974, holds the record for the best-selling American debut for a female solo artist, for her 1995 album *Jagged Little Pill* The album — which won four Grammys, including Album of the Year — has sold more than 33 million copies.

Number One Country

Canadian country music sweetheart Shania Twain, born in Windsor, Ontario, on August 28, 1965, left her mark on the genre. Twain's second album, *The Woman in Me* (1995), holds the record for most weeks at Number One on *Billboard*'s country album chart. It spent 29 weeks at the top and has sold more than 7.7 million copies.

FIRST MILLION-DOLLAR TOUR

April Wine's tour in support of its 1976 album *The Whole World's Goin' Crazy* was the first tour to gross $1 million.

First French Gold Record

Among the many accomplishments of famed songstress Céline Dion, born March 30, 1968, in Charlemagne, Quebec: she was the first Canadian to receive a Gold Record in France. She managed the feat in 1983 at just 15 years old.

Legend of Live

Famed concert promoter Michael Cohl, born in Toronto in 1948, was the first recipient of *Billboard* magazine's Legend of Live award, in November 2004, for his significant contributions to the music touring industry.

Quadruple Platinum

Musician Burton Cummings, born on December 31, 1947, and a member of The Guess Who, was the first Canadian to have a quadruple platinum-selling album in the United States: his 1978 album *Dream Of A Child*.

Five Number One Hits

If you know a teenager or young adult these days, you're likely very familiar with Justin Bieber. Bieber, born in Stratford, Ontario, on March 1, 1994, became the first musician with five Number One albums on the Billboard 200 chart before turning 19 years old. He achieved the feat in early 2013 with his *Believe Acoustic* album. His pervious Number One albums included *Believe* (2012), *Under the Mistletoe* (2011), *Never Say Never: The Remixes* (2011) and *My World 2.0* (2010).

First woman to win Gold Album

Born in Springhill, Nova Scotia, on June 20, 1945, Anne Murray was the first solo Canadian female artist to be awarded an American Gold album (500,000 sales), in 1970, with her second album *This Way is My Way*. It featured the hit "Snowbird."

The most laughs

Its mission statement is simple: "Make people happy." The annual Just for Laughs comedy festival in Montreal is the world's largest, with audiences of nearly two million people each July. The Montreal festival has grown into a major comedy business operation, with festivals in Toronto, Chicago and Sydney, Australia; television shows (*Gags*, seen in 135 countries); live tours and talent management.

Polka king

You could call him Canada's greatest musician, if you use Grammy nominations as the measure. Known as Canada's polka king, Walter Ostanek, born in Duparquet, Quebec, on April 20, 1935, has garnered 21 Grammy nominations over the course of his career. He won three times for Best Polka Album. No other Canadian musician has nabbed as many individual Grammy nominations.

Most naked Canadian

You could say the greatest naked woman of all time is a Canadian. If you count the cover of *Playboy* as the measure, that is. Actress Pamela Anderson, born on July 1, 1967, in Ladysmith, British Columbia, has appeared on the magazine's cover 13 times, more than anyone else.

Most expensive art

During his life, Toronto painter Alex Colville, who died on July 16, 2013 at the age of 92, held the record for the highest price paid for a work of art by a living Canadian artist. "Man on Verandah," painted in 1953, was purchased at an auction on November 25, 2010, for $1.287 million.

Youngest supermodel

Considered Canada's first supermodel, Monika Schnarre, born in Scarborough, Ontario, May 27, 1971, was the youngest person to win the Ford Modeling Agency's Supermodel of the World competition, in 1986 at age 14.

Youngest cover girl

Supermodel Monika Schnarre, was also the youngest person to appear on the cover of *American Vogue* and in *Sports Illustrated*'s swimsuit issue, in 1987 at age 15.

Mr. Grammy

Watching events such as the Grammy Awards on live television is second nature these days. But when television producer Pierre Cossette, born in Valleyfield, Quebec, on December 15, 1923, first suggested the idea in 1970, he had a tough job convincing American network executives. Cossette, now known as "Mr. Grammy," was executive producer of the show for 35 years before he retired.

Top film fest

The Toronto International Film Festival, held annually in September, is considered one of the most important film festivals in the world. It's certainly the premiere festival in North America, and internationally it ranks second, after France's Cannes' festival. It will celebrate its 40th anniversary in 2016.

Top docs fest

Not to be outdone, the Hot Docs Canadian International Documentary Festival is North America's largest documentary festival. Each year during its late April/early May run, Hot Docs presents more than 180 Canadian and international documentary films. The festival was founded in 1993.

Largest Caribbean festival

If you want to celebrate Caribbean culture in Canada, there's nowhere else to be than Toronto in mid-July and early August. The Scotiabank Toronto Caribbean Carnival, formerly Caribana (and still referred to commonly by that moniker), is considered the largest cultural festival of its kind in North America. The highlight of the three-week festival is Parade Day, where Caribbean-inspired acts from around the world celebrate calypso, soca, reggae, hip hop, chutney, steel pan and brass bands.

First film fest

Saskatchewan's Yorkton Film Festival, established as the Yorkton International Film Festival in 1947, was the first film festival in North America. The festival, held each May, was created by James Lysyshyn, a field officer for the National Film Board, and is still going strong today.

Biggest jazz festival

The Montreal International Jazz Festival is considered the largest jazz festival in the world. Held annually in late June/early July since 1982, the modern festival hosts 3,000 musicians from 30 countries, holds more than 1,000 concerts and attracts nearly 2 million visitors.

MOST PRIDE

Toronto was the first city in North America to host the World Pride Festival, an international celebration of lesbian, gay, bisexual, transsexual and transgender individuals. The festival, the fourth ever held, ran June 20 to 29, 2014.

Largest winter carnival

The Quebec Winter Carnival is the largest winter carnival in the world. Held annually from late January through mid-February, the first festival took place in 1894, but the present-day incarnation of the event was established in 1955. The carnival features a variety of winter sports, snow sculptures and activities based on Quebec traditions.

Photo fest

The annual CONTACT Photography Festival is the largest photography event in the world. Held each May in the Greater Toronto Area, it showcases the works of more than 1,500 Canadian and international shutterbugs at at least 175 venues. The festival, which has an estimated audience of 1.8 million, was founded in 1997.

Biggest community event

The Canadian National Exhibition, held each year in Toronto since 1879, is the nation's largest annual community event. The CNE is one of the 10 largest fairs on the continent. It attracted 1.36 million visitors in 2013.

Most maple syrup

Celebrating its 50th anniversary in 2014, the Elmira Maple Syrup Festival, held annually in early April, claims to be the world's largest single-day maple syrup festival (as recognized by Guinness World Records in 2000, when 66,529 people attended the event). The event attracts thousands each year to eat pancakes and sample maple syrup.

Most country music

It's possible they're biased, but Alberta Travel claims the Big Valley Jamboree is the largest outdoor music festival in North America. Held annually in mid-summer since 1993 in Camrose, southeast of Edmonton, the four-day country music fest has hosted a who's who of the genre's top acts.

Biggest agricultural fair

The Royal Agricultural Winter Fair, held annually in November in Toronto, is the largest combined indoor agricultural fair and international equestrian competition in the world. The first Royal opened on November 22, 1922, with 17,000 entries and drew more than 150,000 visitors. Today the fair takes up nearly 93,000 square m of space and attracts thousands of entries and about 300,000 visitors.

Most blooms

Get your garden on. Canada Blooms is the largest flower and garden festival in Canada. Held annually in March since 1997, the exhibition now attracts more than 200,000 visitors. Among many exhibits are fantasy gardens created by the world's top designers.

First agricultural fair

The first agricultural fair in North America was held in Windsor, Nova Scotia, in May 1765. The Hants County Exhibition still takes place each September, making it the oldest, continuously run agricultural exhibition on the continent.

Most outdoor musicals

Winnipeg's Rainbow Stage, a musical theatre company that performs in the city's Kildonan Park, is the nation's largest and longest-running outdoor theatre. The company's 3,000-seat amphitheatre opened on July 7, 1954, and the first musical, *Brigadoon*, was performed in 1955. Today the Rainbow Stage attracts more than 40,000 patrons annually.

Biggest Fringe

The Edmonton International Fringe Theatre Festival was the first such festival and it is the largest in North America and the second-largest in the world. It's been held each August since 1982.

Most Elvis

Elvis lives! At least he does at the Collingwood Elvis Festival, held each July since 1995. It's the world's largest festival celebrating legendary singer Elvis Presley. The highlight of the event is the Elvis impersonator contest, which attracts many of the world's best Elvis tribute artists.

Biggest tattoo

Billed as the world's largest annual indoor show, the Royal Nova Scotia International Tattoo is held annually during the first week of July and features a variety of entertainment, including bagpipes, highland dancers, military displays, acrobats and more. The Tattoo has been held yearly since 1979.

Biggest children's theatre

Toronto's Young People's Theatre is the largest theatre for young audiences in the nation. It was established in 1966 by Susan Douglas Rubes, and the first production was *The Looking Glass Revue*, which was aimed at children aged 3 to 7. Since the start, the theatre has been dedicated to productions written specifically for children.

First theatre production

The first European theatrical production in North America was performed in Port-Royal, Nova Scotia, in 1606. French poet and playwright Marc Lescarbot presented *Théâtre de Neptune*.

First Canadian play

Acadius, the story of a wealthy Boston businessman's extramarital affairs and how his black servants dealt with their exploitation, is considered the first original Canadian play. It was performed in Halifax in 1774, and its author is unknown.

Most theatres

Toronto has the largest variety of theatres and performing arts companies in Canada, the second-largest in North America after New York City, and the third-largest in the world after London, England. Ten major theatres host the likes of the Canadian Opera Company, the National Ballet of Canada and Mirvish and DanCap Productions, two large private entertainment companies.

Oldest ballet company

The Royal Winnipeg Ballet is the nation's oldest dance company and the second-oldest in North America. Founded as the Winnipeg Ballet Club by Gweneth Lloyd and Betty Farrally, the organization gave its first performance in 1939. The club received a royal charter from Queen Elizabeth II in 1953 to become the first "Royal" ballet company of the Commonwealth.

Largest opera company

The Canadian Opera Company was the nation's first opera company, and it is the largest. It began as the Canadian Opera Festival in February 1950, and today the COC attracts about 140,000 patrons each season.

First radio symphony concert series

Businessman Henry Thornton inaugurated the first radio transcontinental symphonic series in North America on October 20, 1929. The "All-Canada Symphony Concerts" were performed by 55 members of the Toronto Symphony Orchestra and culminated on April 6, 1930, in a concert entirely of Canadian-composed music.

First symphony

The Quebec Symphony Orchestra, based in Quebec City, is the oldest symphony in Canada. It was officially formed on October 3, 1902, and gave its first performance on November 28 that year. Today, the orchestra attracts an audience of about 100,000 annually.

First opera school

The opera school founded by Canada's Royal Conservatory of Music (known as the Toronto Conservatory of Music at the time) in 1946 was the nation's first school dedicated to the professional training of singers.

First Canadian opera

Canada's first original operatic work was composed by Louis-Joseph-Marie Quesnel. *Colas et Colinette* was first performed in Montreal in 1970.

Largest classical theatre

Stratford, Ontario, hosts the largest classical repertory theatre in North America. Founded in 1953, the Stratford Festival presents numerous shows spring through fall annually at four theatres in the town. In 2013, the festival attracted 480,000 patrons.

First orchestra concert for children

In 1924–25, its second season, the Toronto Symphony Orchestra performed the first orchestra concert specifically for children. The performance was part of the orchestra's efforts to engage and attract a younger audience.

FIRST CANADIAN PUBLISHED ORCHESTRAL WORK

The first Canadian orchestral composition to be published was Guillaume Couture's *Rêverie*, which was performed in Paris in 1875 and then published.

FIRST NATIONAL BALLET *GISELLE*

The National Ballet of Canada (NBC) was formed in 1951. Its first performance was *Giselle* (considered the *Hamlet* of dance) on November 12 of that year at Toronto's Eaton Auditorium. The ballet has been performed many times since then by the NBC, which is one of the few ballet companies that has always had its own orchestra.

First diva

Emma Albani, born Marie-Louise-Emma-Cécile Lajeunesse on November 1, 1847, in Chambly, Quebec, was the first Canadian opera singer to attain international success. She was a sought-after performer by opera enthusiasts in France, Italy, England, Mexico and Australia.

First Canadian orchestral work played in Europe

The first Canadian orchestral work to be performed in Europe is thought to be *Patrie*, written by Calixa Lavallée (also the composer of *O Canada*). It was performed in 1874.

FIRST HOCKEY GAME

Hockey is so popular in Canada that a number of Canadian cities claim to have hosted the first game, if not invented the game outright (such as Halifax; Windsor, Nova Scotia; and Kingston, Ontario). Regardless, one of the first reliable records of a form of the game being played is from a journal of Arctic explorer John Franklin, who notes a game on Great Bear Lake at Fort Franklin, Northwest Territories, on October 25, 1825.

First indoor hockey game

The first record of a hockey game played on an indoor ice rink between two teams was on March 3, 1875. It took place at Victoria Skating Rink in Montreal. It's thought that the game as we know it was formed in Montreal according to rules developed by George Aylwin Creighton.

First Olympic gold for hockey

The Winnipeg Falcons were the first team to win an Olympic gold medal in hockey, in 1920 in Antwerp, Belgium. At the time, the winner of the Allan Cup, awarded to the nation's top senior men's amateur hockey club, was selected to represent the country at the games. The Falcons dominated the tournament, besting Czechoslovakia 15-0, the United States 2-0 and Sweden 12-1 to claim gold. At the time the event was held in the summer.

Best hockey player

Wayne Gretzky — 'nuff said! But if you need more, the man who many consider to be the greatest hockey player ever holds or shares 61 records in the National Hockey League. Some highlights:

Most points: 2,856 (1,485 games, 894 goals, 1,962 assists)
Most points, including playoffs: 3,238 (2,856 regular season, 382 playoff)
Most goals: 894
Most goals, including playoffs: 1,016 (894 regular season, 122 playoff)
Most assists: 1,962
Most assists, including playoffs: 2,222 (1,962 regular season, 260 playoff)
Most consecutive 40-or-more-goal seasons: 12 (1979–80 to 1990–91)
Most consecutive 60-or-more-goal seasons: 4 (1981–82 to 1984–85)
Most consecutive 100-or-more-point seasons: 13 (1979–80 to 1991–92)

Single Season Records

Most points, one season: 215 (1985–86, 80-game schedule)
Most points, one season, including playoffs: 255 (1984–85; 208 points in 80 regular- season games and 47 points in 18 playoff games)
Most goals, one season: 92 (1981–82, 80-game schedule)
Most goals, one season, including playoffs: 100 (1983–84, 87 goals in 74 regular-season games and 13 goals in 19 playoff games)
Most goals, 50 games from start of season: 61 (1981–82 and 1983–84)
Most three-or-more-goal games: 10 (1981–82, six three-goal games; three four-goal games; one five-goal game)
Longest consecutive point-scoring streak: 51 games — 61 goals, 92 assists for 153 points (October 5, 1983, to January 28, 1984)

Career Records: Playoffs

Most playoff goals: 122
Most playoff assists: 260
Most playoff points: 382 (122 goals, 260 assists)
Most game-winning goals in playoffs: 24
Most points, one playoff year: 47 (1985, 17 goals and 30 assists in 18 games)
Most points in final series: 13 — three goals and 10 assists (1988, four games plus suspended game vs. Boston)

First radio hockey

"He shoots, he scores!" While it's still a matter of debate, the Hockey Hall of Fame reports that the very first radio broadcast of a hockey game took place on February 16, 1923. Legendary announcer Foster Hewitt called the action of the game between Kitchener and Toronto at the Arena Gardens on Toronto station CFCA.

First to score 500 goals

Maurice "Rocket" Richard, who played his entire career for the Montreal Canadiens, was the first professional hockey player to score 50 goals in 50 games (in 1945–46), but he was also the first professional to score 500 career goals (he tallied his 500th on October 19, 1957). When Richard retired, he'd scored 544 goals.

First goalie mask

The first person known to wear a goalie mask in a hockey game? Bet you didn't know it was Elizabeth Graham. In 1927, Graham used a fencing mask to protect her face.

First professional goalie mask

The first professional hockey player to wear a goalie mask was Clint Benedict. Benedict, who played for the Montreal Maroons, is believed to have worn a mask for a game or two in 1929.

Million-dollar hockey player

Bobby Hull was the first hockey player to sign a $1 million-dollar contract. He accepted the contract with the Winnipeg Jets, then part of the World Hockey Association, on June 27, 1972, at the corner of Portage and Main in Winnipeg.

First tabletop hockey

The tabletop hockey game was invented in 1932 by Toronto's Don Munro. A bump in the middle of the wooden board kept the steel ball moving, while one lever controlled the goalie and another controlled the other players. Versions of his game were popular until 1954, when a competitor introduced players printed in colour on flat tin cutouts.

First father and son in Hockey Hall of Fame

Bobby Hull and his son Brett became the first father and son inducted into the Hockey Hall of Fame, when Brett joined the Hall on November 9, 2009. Brett recorded 1,391 points in 1,269 regular-season games. Bobby tallied 1,170 points in 1,063 regular-season games.

Popularizing the goalie mask

Usually one too many shots to the head does not lead to innovation. But for Canadian Jacques Plante, goaltender for the Montreal Canadiens, getting hit in the face by one more puck on November 1, 1959, was the last straw. After getting stitched up, Plante returned to the game wearing a mask and began the popularization of the equipment.

First Winter Olympic games

While it wasn't technically referred to as such, the 1924 International Winter Sports Week, organized by the International Olympic Committee and held in Chamonix, France, is widely considered the first Winter Olympic Games. It could be said that Canada won its first Winter Olympic medal at the event — gold in hockey (the 1920 gold in hockey had been won at the summer games).

First state funeral

Maurice Richard holds a very unique distinction for a Canadian athlete. After his death on May 27, 2000, Richard was given a state funeral by his home province of Quebec, which was broadcast live across the country — the first time such an honour was bestowed on a Canadian athlete.

DEFENCEMAN TOP SCORES

Bobby Orr, born in Parry Sound, Ontario, on March 20, 1948, is the only defenceman to lead the National Hockey League in regular-season scoring. Orr accomplished the feat twice, in 1969–70 (120 points) and in 1974–75 (122 points).

Most traded players

These guys have a lot of sweaters in their closets. Canadian hockey players Mike Sillinger and Brent Aston are tied for the most-traded National Hockey League player. Each was traded nine times during his career.

COACH WITH THE MOST STANLEY CUPS

Legendary hockey coach Scotty Bowman, born in Montreal on September 18, 1933, has won more Stanley Cups than any other coach. His nine championships — five with Montreal (1973, 1976, 1977, 1978 1979), one with Pittsburgh (1992) and three with Detroit (1997, 1998 and 2002) — also tie him with basketball coach Red Auerbach for the most championships in North America's four major pro sports leagues.

First black hockey player

Willie O'Ree was the first black player in the National Hockey League. His first game was January 18, 1958. O'Ree, born in Fredericton on October 15, 1935, played two seasons for the Boston Bruins (1957–58 and 1960–61) and scored four goals and tallied 10 assists.

The oldest sports trophy

The Stanley Cup, which is awarded to the champion of the National Hockey League, is the oldest trophy competed for by professional athletes in North America. The trophy was established in 1892 by Sir Frederick Arthur Stanley (Lord Stanley), to be presented to the top hockey club in the Dominion of Canada. NHL teams became the exclusive competitors for the Cup in 1926.

Engraving the Stanley Cup

Engraving the names of the winning team's roster on the Stanley Cup has become a tradition. But the custom only began in 1907, when the Montreal Wanderers became the first to do so. It wasn't until 1924 that the ritual was performed annually.

Last Canadian Stanley Cup

As of this writing, the Montreal Canadians were the last Canadian team to win the Stanley Cup, in 1993. The city has a long tradition of capturing the Cup. Its Montreal AAA team was awarded the trophy the first time it was presented, in 1893. Indeed, it won the championship in each of its first eight years.

Team with the most Cups

The Montreal Canadiens have hoisted the Stanley Cup more than any other team in the trophy's history. The team has won the Cup 24 times, first in 1916 and most recently in 1993.

National summer sport

While many consider hockey Canada's national sport — and the federal government named it the country's national winter sport — lacrosse is considered the national summer sport. It's believed the game has been around for centuries, played in North America long before Europeans arrived. People have speculated that Native Americans invented the game as long ago as the 12th century.

Run of eight world championships

Talk about a sports dynasty. The first eight women's World Hockey Championship tournaments were won by Canada. Canada beat the American team in each championship game, from the inaugural tournament in Ottawa in 1990 to the Halifax/Dartmouth event in 2004. (The 2003 tournament slated for Beijing, China, was cancelled.)

First sports association

The National Lacrosse Association was Canada's first sports association. It was established on September 26, 1867, in Kingston, Ontario.

FIRST SPORT CLUB

The first sporting club in Canada was the Montreal Curling Club, which was founded in 1807.

Longest-running television sports program

Television trivia time. Name the longest-running sports program in television history. It's CBC's *Hockey Night in Canada*. The show made its television debut (the brand has been on the radio since 1933) on October 11, 1952, airing a game between the Montreal Canadiens and the Detroit Red Wings. HNIC has broadcast a regular-season National Hockey League game every Saturday night since.

Fastest ice

It's hardly surprising that the so-called "fastest ice in the world" is in Canada. Specifically, it's at the Olympic Oval in Calgary, built for the 1988 Winter Olympic Games. It's earned the honour thanks to the 258 long track and 30 short track world records set on the surface. Why so quick? The ice is made with demineralized water, which reduces the amount of dirt and mineral buildup that can create friction between ice and skate. Less friction equals faster ice. The track was also the first fully covered 400 m oval in North America.

World's largest skating rink

Where else but Canada's capital would you find the world's largest skating rink? Located on the Rideau Canal in downtown Ottawa, the Skateway is 7.8 km long, running from near the Parliament Buildings to Dow's Lake. It's typically open January through February, with the average season lasting 50 days. Its first season of 1971–72 set a record of 90 days.

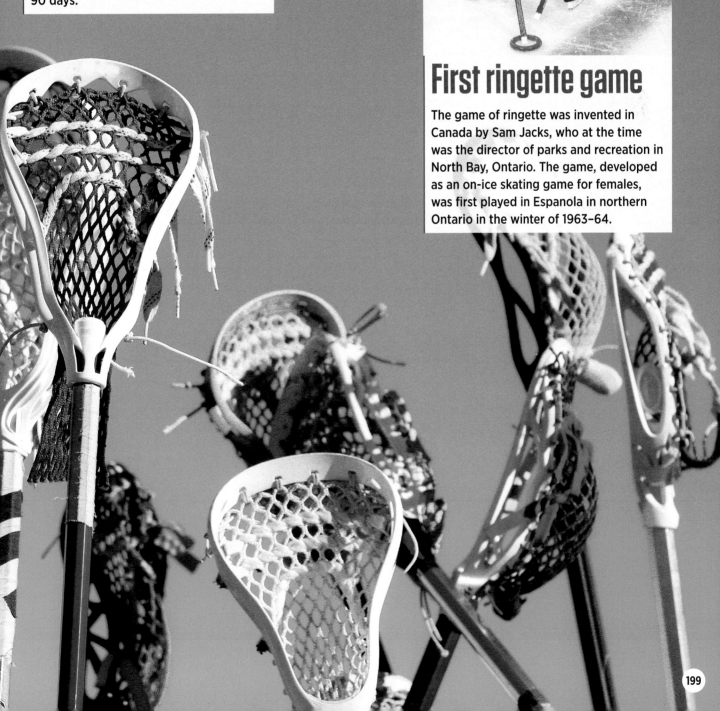

First ringette game

The game of ringette was invented in Canada by Sam Jacks, who at the time was the director of parks and recreation in North Bay, Ontario. The game, developed as an on-ice skating game for females, was first played in Espanola in northern Ontario in the winter of 1963–64.

First Triple Crown

In 1919, Canadian-owned racehorse Sir Barton was the first to win the American Triple Crown—capturing first in each of the Kentucky Derby, Preakness and Belmont Stakes races — although the title didn't exist at the time. Sir Barton, owned by J.K.L. Ross, was officially awarded the honour in 1948.

Oldest horse race

The Queen's Plate, held annually since 1860, is the oldest continuously run horse race in North America. Today, it's run each July at Toronto's Woodbine Racetrack. The race has been attended by reigning monarchs five times in its history, and by representatives of the monarchy another dozen times.

First Canadian to win Derby

Racehorse Northern Dancer, born in Oshawa, Ontario, on May 27, 1961, was the first Canadian-bred horse to win the Kentucky Derby, in 1964. Northern Dancer also won the Preakness Stakes in the same year.

Oldest sporting event

Here's betting you didn't know that the Royal St. John's Regatta is the oldest sporting event in North America. It's also known as "the largest garden party in the world," thanks to the socializing that accompanies the rowing races. The first record of the event is from 1818, however, crews were known to compete in the St. John's Harbour since the 1700s. Today, the event, held annually in August, draws 50,000 spectators to the shores of Quidi Vidi Lake.

FIRST YACHT CLUB

The Royal Halifax Yacht Club was the first yacht club in North America. Its beginnings date back to July 1837, though it wasn't officially established as the RHYC until 1861. In 1922, the club became the Royal Nova Scotia Yacht Squadron.

Jockey wins 500 +

Jockey Sandy Hawley, born in Oshawa, Ontario, on April 16, 1949, was the first to win 500 races in one year. Hawley eclipsed the record in 1973, totaling 515 first-place finishes. During his career, Hawley won 6,449 races, and stands eighth among jockeys for the most career wins.

First NBA game

The first National Basketball Association game was played in Canada. On November 1, 1946, the New York Knickerbockers beat the Toronto Huskies 68 to 66 at Toronto's Maple Leaf Gardens.

Basket Ball.

The ball to be an ordinary Association foot ball.

1. The ball may be thrown in any direction with one or both hands.

2. The ball may be batted in any direction with one or both hands (never with the fist).

3. A player cannot run with the ball, the player must throw it from the spot on which he catches it, allowance to be made for a man who catches the ball when running at a good speed.

4. The ball must be held in or between the hands, the arms or body must not be used for holding it.

5. No shouldering, holding, pushing, tripping or striking in any way the person of an opponent shall be allowed. The first infringement of this rule by any person shall count as a foul, the second shall disqualify him until the next goal is made, or if there was evident intent to injure the person, for the whole of the game, no substitute allowed.

6. A foul is striking at the ball with the fist, violation of rules 3 and 4, and such as described in rule 5.

7. If either side makes three consecutive fouls it shall count a goal for the opponents (consecutive means without the opponents in the meantime making a foul).

8. A goal shall be made when the ball is thrown or batted from the grounds into the basket and stays there, providing those defending the goal do not touch or disturb the goal. If the ball rests on the edge and the opponent moves the basket it shall count as a

Canadian basketball

When it comes to quintessential Canadian sports, basketball doesn't immediately spring to mind. But the sport was invented by a Canadian, Dr. James Naismith, who was born November 6, 1861, in Almonte, Ontario. He came up with the game in 1891 and it was first played on December 21 of that year at Springfield College in Massachusetts.

Double whammy

Hank Biasatti is the only Canadian to play at the major league level in both basketball and baseball. Aside from playing with basketball's Toronto Huskies in 1946, Biasatti played professional baseball for the Philadelphia Athletics in 1949.

First Canadian MVP

Steve Nash was the first Canadian to win the Most Valuable Player award in the National Basketball Association. Nash, a Vancouver native born on February 7, 1974, captured the award in the 2004–2005 season, then again the following year. He was only the ninth player in the league's history to win back-to-back MVP awards and only the third guard to win the award multiple times.

Greatest basketball team

James Naismith called the Edmonton Grads "the finest basketball team that ever stepped out on a floor." Between 1915 and 1940, The Edmonton Commercial Graduates, a women's team often referred to as the greatest basketball team ever, played 522 games the world over and won 502, including 147 straight victories. The Grads also won seven of nine games against men's teams.

First Olympic gold

George W. Orton of Strathroy, Ontario, won the nation's first Olympic gold medal at the Paris games in 1900, despite the fact that Canada did not send a team to the event. Orton was asked to join the American team, thanks to his many victories at track and field meets throughout the United States, and he reached the top of the podium in the 2,500 m steeplechase. He also won bronze in the 400 m hurdles at the games.

First Olympic team

The 1904 Olympic Games in St. Louis marked the first time Canada sent an official team to the event. The 43-member team won six medals: four gold, a silver and a bronze. The gold medals came in soccer, lacrosse, 56-pound weight throw and golf.

FIRST GOLD AND SILVER IN SAME EVENT

The 1908 Olympic Games in London, England, marked the first time Canada captured gold and silver in the same event. Walter Ewing and George Beattie took first and second in the clay pigeon event.

Multiple medals

There are few athletes that reach the pinnacle of multiple sports. Canadian Olympic athlete Clara Hughes, however, is one of the world's finest exceptions. Hughes is the only Olympian ever to win multiple medals at summer and winter games. In speed skating she captured gold in the 5,000 m and silver in the team pursuit at the games in Turin, Italy, in 2006. As a cyclist, Hughes won bronze in both the road race and time trial events in Atlanta in 1996.

First female Olympic shooter

Born in Medicine Hat, Alberta, on November 5, 1950, Susan Natrass was the first woman to ever compete in the Olympics in a shooting event (shooting was open to both sexes until 1992). She placed 25th in the trap event at the 1976 Games in Montreal.

MOST MEDALS AT ONE OLYMPICS

Cindy Klassen (see right) holds the Canadian record for winning the most medals (five) at one Olympic Games. She reached the podium in the following long-track speed skating events in Turin, Italy in 2006: 1,000 m, 1,500 m, 3,000 m, 5,000 m and team pursuit. Her haul is also the most ever won by a female speed skater.

First individual gold

Speed skater Gaétan Boucher, born in Charlesbourg, Quebec, on May 10, 1958, was the first Canadian man to win an individual gold medal at the Winter Olympic Games. In fact, he won two gold medals (one in 1,000 m and one in 1,500 m) on February 14, 1984, in Sarajevo, Bosnia and Herzegovina.

Most medals

Clara Hughes (see right) and fellow speed skater Cindy Klassen are tied as the most-decorated Canadian Olympians. Each won six medals: Hughes captured four bronze (two in speed skating, two in cycling), one silver and one gold (both speed skating); Klassen nabbed three bronze, two silver and one gold, all in speed skating.

First Canadian World Series win

In 1992, the Toronto Blue Jays became the first non-American team to win baseball's World Series championship. They defeated the Atlanta Braves on October 24 to claim the title. The team repeated the feat in 1993.

Baseball's mysterious origins

So baseball is America's game, eh? Explain this: a year before the game's accepted creator Abner Doubleday is credited with founding the sport, the first recorded baseball game in North America took place in Beachville, Ontario. Teams from Oxford and Zorra townships played on June 4, 1838.

First Canadian pro ballplayer

You've got to look back nearly 150 years to find the record of the first Canadian to play professional baseball. William B. (Bill) Phillips, born in Saint John in 1857, played his first game for the National League's Cleveland Blues on May 1, 1879. The first baseman also played for the league's Brooklyn Grays and Kansas City Cowboys, with a total of 1,881 games played.

FIRST CANADIAN CY YOUNG AWARD

You could call him the ace of Canadian aces. Baseball pitcher Ferguson Jenkins, born in Chatham, Ontario, on December 12, 1942, was the first Canadian to win the Cy Young Award, awarded annually to the game's best pitcher. Jenkins nabbed the honour while pitching for the Chicago Cubs in 1971, and played for four other clubs before retiring in 1983.

Babe Ruth's first pro homer

Legendary baseball player Babe Ruth hit his first professional home run in Toronto. On September 5, 1914, as a 19-year-old rookie in the International League, Ruth hit that monumental homer at Maple Leaf Park on the Toronto Islands.

FIRST CANADIAN TEAM IN MAJOR LEAGUE BASEBALL

The Montreal Expos were the first Canadian team to join Major League Baseball, in 1969. In 2004, the team was relocated to Washington, D.C. and renamed the Washington Nationals.

First Canadian in Baseball Hall of Fame

Pitcher Ferguson Jenkins was the first Canadian elected to the American National Baseball Hall of Fame in Cooperstown, New York, in 1987. Jenkins won 284 games — including a stretch of 20 a year for six straight seasons — and is the only pitcher in the game's history to strike out more than 3,000 batters and walk less than 1,000 batters.

Invention of 5-pin bowling

The invention of 5-pin bowling, a Canadian concept, was the result of dissatisfaction with the American, 10-pin version of the game. Thomas F. (Tommy) Ryan opened the first regulation 10-pin lanes in Toronto in 1905, but customers complained about the size and weight of the balls. Ryan began experimenting with different pin and ball sizes, and in 1909, Canada's superior 5-pin game was born.

First black ballplayer

Jackie Robinson, the first black baseball player in Major League Baseball in the modern era, played his first professional games for the Montreal Royals in 1946. A minor-league affiliate of the Brooklyn Dodgers — the team Robinson would debut with in majors — the Royals won the International League title that season.

First Commonwealth Games

In 1930, Hamilton, Ontario, was the first host of the British Empire Games, which eventually became the Commonwealth Games. Participating nations included Australia, Bermuda, British Guyana, England, Northern Ireland, Newfoundland, New Zealand, South Africa and Wales. The games featured six sports: athletics, boxing, lawn bowls, rowing, swimming and diving, and wrestling.

Crazy Canuck Championship win

Another Crazy Canuck, Steve Podborski of Toronto, was the first male non-European skier to win the World Cup Downhill Championship, which he accomplished in 1982. Over his career, Podborski captured eight World Cup race wins and a bronze medal in downhill at the Lake Placid Olympics in 1980.

Crazy Canuck World Cup win

Considered the leader of the Crazy Canucks, Canada's team of top competitive skiers of the 1970s and 1980s, Ken Read was the first non-European to win a World Cup downhill race. Read, who calls Calgary home, achieved the milestone in Val d'Isere, France in 1975.

Biggest ski resort

If you're looking for a ski run, look no further than Alberta's Lake Louise Ski Resort, the nation's largest, and one of the biggest on the continent. The resort boasts 4,200 skiable areas, 145 named runs and 10 lifts. The resort's longest run is 8 km.

Ski on a glacier

The Whistler Blackcomb Ski Resort, in Whistler, British Columbia, is the only ski resort in North America where you can ski or ride on a glacier. The Horstman Glacier is typically open to skiing through June and July, helping Whistler Blackcomb achieve the country's longest ski season.

First World Ski winner

Skier Lucile Wheeler, born on January 14, 1935, in St-Jovite, Quebec, was the first North American to win a World Ski Championship. She captured first in both downhill and giant slalom at the events in Bad Gastein, Austria, in February 1958. She was also the first Canadian to win a medal in downhill at the Olympics — bronze in 1956 at Cortina d'Ampezzo, Italy.

First alpine gold

Anne Heggtveit, born in Ottawa on January 11, 1939, won Canada's first-ever gold medal in alpine skiing, which was also the first North American gold in slalom. She captured the medal at the 1960 Olympic Games in Squaw Valley, California.

First female golf club members

A progressive first: The Royal Montreal Golf Club was the first golf club in North America to allow female members.

Longest luge

The Skyline Calgary luge track is the world's longest, at 1.8 km. The warm-weather track, which uses wheeled sleds, drops more than 100 m over its entire length. Located at the city's Winsport Olympic Park, the summer track runs along the luge course built for the 1988 Winter Games.

Longest golf hole

Fore! Actually, perhaps that's not necessary on Canada's longest golf hole. The 11th hole at The Nursery Golf and Country Club near Lacombe, Alberta, is a whopping 782 yards! The course's hole description notes: "Your first two shots are critical…" Indeed.

Oldest golf club

The Royal Montreal Golf Club is the oldest golf club in North America. Formed as the Montreal Golf Club in 1873 (it received the Royal designation in 1884), the first course was nine holes on Fletcher's Field, part of Mount Royal Park on the outskirts of Montreal.

Strongest man in the world

Before weightlifting was a formal sport, Canadian Louis Cyr, born in Saint-Cyprien-de-Napierville, Quebec, on October 10, 1863, was considered one of the strongest men in the world. He was undefeated in lifting competitions, capturing the weightlifting championship of North America in 1885 and the world title in 1892.

Toughest boxer

None other than Muhammad Ali, considered the greatest heavyweight boxer ever, called Canadian boxer George Chuvalo "the toughest man I ever fought." Chuvalo, born on September 12, 1937, in Toronto, was the sport's Canadian heavyweight champion from September 1958 until he retired in 1979. While he never captured the world title, in 97 professional matches, Chuvalo was never knocked out or down — even in two losses to Ali.

First quadruple jump

He put a whole new spin on things. In 1988, at the World Figure Skating Championships in Budapest, Hungry, Kurt Browning, born in Rocky Mountain House, Alberta, on June 18, 1966, performed the first quadruple jump in competition in the sport's history. Oh, he won the championship, too.

First cereal box appearance

Bet you'll never guess who was the first Canadian athlete to appear on the front of an American cereal box. Did you know it was Kurt Browning (see above)? Figure skater Browning graced the front of Special K boxes in 1998.

First double Lutz

Figure skater Barbara Ann Scott, born in Ottawa in 1928, was the first woman to land a double Lutz jump in competition in 1942. The feat helped her capture the gold medal at the 1948 Winter Olympics in St. Moritz, Switzerland. Scott was also the first non-European to win a world championship in skating in 1947.

First death spiral

Canadian figure skating duo Suzanne Morrow and Wallace Distelmeyer were the first team to execute the modern-day death spiral in an international competition. They performed the move at the 1948 World Figure Skating Championships in Davos, Switzerland.

First triple Lutz

Don Jackson of Oshawa, Ontario, was the first person to land a triple Lutz jump in competition. He performed the feat on March 15, 1962, at the World Figure Skating Championship in Prague, Czech Republic. It was another 12 years before the jump was repeated in competition.

World Heavyweight Boxing Champion

He's Canada's only world heavyweight boxing champion. Tommy Burns, born in Hanover, Ontario, on June 17, 1881, won the world title on February 23, 1906, in a 20-round decision over Marvin Hart in Los Angeles. He held the championship until December 26, 1908, when he was defeated by Jack Johnson — the first black fighter to hold the world heavyweight title — in 14 rounds in Sydney, Australia.

Largest fitness club company

GoodLife Fitness, a fitness club company, is the largest in the nation. Established in 1979, it has more than 877,000 members who visit its 300-plus clubs across the country.

First perfect seven

That first triple Lutz performed by Don Jackson (see First triple lutz, left) wasn't his only amazing "first." At the end of his performance at the 1962 championship where he unveiled the triple Lutz, Jackson received seven perfect scores (6.0) from the judges, the highest tally ever.

First World Figure Skating Championship

Don Jackson wasn't done there. His perfect score won him the 1962 World Figure Skating Championship, and made him the first Canadian man to do so.

Fastest bike relay across Canada

The fastest cycling relay across Canada, according to Guinness World Records, is 8 days, 8 hours and 14 minutes. A team of five Canadians — Matt Young, Kyle Bagnano, Willie Cormack, Richard Alm and Keith Nicoll — set the record between September 4 and 22, 2007, cycling from Halifax to Vancouver. Their average speed? Forty km per hour.

First wheelchair gold in non-disabled competition

Chantal Petitclerc, born December 15, 1969, holds a truly unique athletic distinction. Petitclerc was the first athlete to claim gold in a wheelchair event as part of a major international non-disabled competition. She captured top spot in the 800 m event in July 2002 at the Commonwealth Games in Manchester, England.

First concussion sensors in high school

There's no shortage of concussion talk these days in sports. And thankfully, lots of experts are doing their best to prevent the head injuries. In the fall of 2013, Calgary's Ernest Manning High School became the first secondary school in Canada to install specifically designed sensors (called the "Shockbox") in their helmets to measure the impact of collisions. Calgary's Canadian Football League team, the Stampeders, were the first pigskin club in the country to employ the device.

Fastest cyclist

A native of Quadra Island, British Columbia, Sam Whittingham is considered the fastest bicyclist in the world. He holds five cycling speed records from the World Human Powered Vehicle Association and shares another. His fastest speed was recorded on September 18, 2009, at Battle Mountain, Nevada, when he clocked 133.28 km per hour in the men's 200 m flying start.

Fastest bike ride across Canada

Here's a long, fast bike ride. According to Guinness World Records, the fastest time to cycle across Canada is 13 days, 6 hours and 13 minutes. Canadian Arvid Loewen set the mark between July 1 and 14, 2011, travelling 6,037 km from Vancouver to Halifax.

Toughest sled dog race

The Yukon Quest 1,000 Mile International Sled Dog Race, is the self-proclaimed "toughest sled dog race in the world." The 1,600 km competition runs each February between Whitehorse, Yukon, and Fairbanks, Alaska, along the historical Klondike gold rush route. Besides the great distance, racers face temperatures plunging to −40°C, winds up to 160 km per hour and steep mountain summits.

Oldest marathon run

When it comes to legendary road running races, one thinks of Boston and New York. But Hamilton, Ontario? One should, as it's home to the oldest marathon in North America (preceding Boston's by three years), the Around the Bay Road Race, which was first run in 1894. The 30 km race has been won by the best in the world, including Olympic medalists and Boston Marathon winners.

First Canadian to win Boston marathon

Thomas Longboat, born on July 4, 1887, in Six Nations, Ontario, was the first Canadian to win the Boston Marathon, the world's oldest annual marathon (it was first run in 1897). Longboat won the legendary race in 1907.

First Canadian to climb Everest

Talk about the height of sports. Laurie Skreslet, born in Calgary on October 25, 1949, was the first Canadian to climb to the summit of Mount Everest, the world's tallest peak. He did it on his 33rd birthday, October 5, 1982.

First Western woman to climb Everest

Another Canadian also set a significant milestone on Everest (see left). Sharon Wood, born in Halifax on May 18, 1957, was the first woman from the Western Hemisphere to reach the summit of Mount Everest. She completed the climb on May 20, 1986.

Canada's first fastest man

He was Canada's first recorded fastest man: Harry Winston Jerome, born on September 30, 1940, in Prince Albert, Saskatchewan, was the first Canadian to officially hold a world track record. In 1960, at just 19, Jerome ran the 100 m in 10 seconds at the Canadian Olympic Trials to tie the world mark. Jerome held several sprinting world records through his career.

Fastest run across Canada (man)

The fastest trip across Canada on foot by a man (Al Howie of England), took 72 days, 10 hours and 23 minutes, according to Guinness World Records. The 7,295.5 km trek from St. John's to Victoria took place from June 21 to September 1, 1991.

Fastest run across Canada (woman)

The fastest trip across Canada on foot by a woman (Canadian Ann Keane), took 143 days. According to Guinness World Records, Keane travelled 7,831 km from St. John's to Tofino, British Columbia between April 17 and September 8, 2002.

Tennis champ extraordinaire

He's a tennis virtuoso. Daniel Nestor, born on September 4, 1972, is the only player in the game's history to win all four Grand Slams, all of the Master Series events, the year-end Masters Cup and an Olympic gold medal in doubles.

First swim across Lake Ontario

You could call it the first great lake swim. Marilyn Bell, born in Toronto on November 19, 1937, was the first person to swim across Lake Ontario. At just 16 years old, Bell completed the swim from Youngstown, New York, to Toronto on September 9, 1954. It took her 20 hours and 59 minutes to swim the estimated 51.5 km course.

Youngest to swim English Channel

Marilyn Bell was the youngest person to swim the English Channel. She achieved that feat on July 31, 1955, at the age of 17.

First to swim the English Channel both ways

There must be something in the water near Toronto. Cindy Nicholas, born on August 20, 1957, in Ontario's capital, was the first woman to swim the English Channel both ways non-stop. She accomplished the record swim on September 8, 1977, in 19 hours and 55 minutes.

Youngest to swim Juan de Fuca Strait

One more long-distance swimming mark for Marilyn Bell (see left): on August 23, 1956, Bell became the youngest person to swim across British Columbia's Juan de Fuca Strait. She completed the crossing in 10 hours and 39 minutes, after which she retired from marathon swimming.

First synchronized swimming competition

Ornamental swimming, anyone? Montreal hosted the first synchronized swimming competition ever — called ornamental or figure swimming at the time — in 1924. The event was a provincial championship, which was won by Peg Seller, who was also a top Canadian diver and water polo player.

First Canadian Grand Prix win

Race car driver Gilles Villeneuve, born on January 18, 1950, in Chambly, Quebec, was the first Canadian to win a Grand Prix event. Villeneuve won the Formula One in Montreal, the Canadian Grand Prix, on October 8, 1978. The track is now named after him. Villeneuve died in a crash during a qualifying session for the Belgium Grand Prix on May 8, 1982.

First Canadian Grand Prix

Formula One cars first raced in Canada at the inaugural Canadian Grand Prix on August 27, 1967, at the Mosport racetrack — today called the Canadian Tire Motorsport Park — in Bowmanville, Ontario. Jack Brabham of Australia won that first race.

First official document

The first and oldest known official document from what is modern-day Canada, is the pardon of Aussillon de Sauveterre, who had killed a sailor. The pardon was granted in September 1542, by Jean-François de La Rocque de Roberval, Canada's lieutenant-general at the time.

First European flag in Canada

The first recorded European flag to fly in North America had the flag of England on one side and the winged-lion pennant of St. Mark of Venice on the opposite side. It flew on St. John's Island (present-day Prince Edward Island) on June 24, 1497, planted by the crew of John Cabot.

First secret session of parliament

Keep it on the down low. On April 17, 1918, the House of Commons held its first secret session. Members were told that Allied forces in Europe faced possible defeat.

First province where women could vote

Manitoba was the first province in Canada to grant woman the right to vote, in 1916. First proposed by Manitoba's Icelandic community in the 1870s, the fight for women's suffrage was taken up by a team of women, including Dr. Mary Crawford, Lillian Beynon Thomas and Nellie McClung.

First Order of Canada recipients

The Order of Canada, created in 1967 in honour of the 100th anniversary of Confederation, is awarded to Canadians who demonstrate exemplary merit and achievement. Ninety people were appointed, including:

- Governor General Roland Michener, the first honourary member
- Montreal Symphony conductor Wilfrid Pelletier
- Quebec politician Thérèse Casgrain
- Author Hugh MacLennan
- Humourist Gregory Clark
- Neurosurgeon Dr. Wilder Penfield
- Former Prime Minister Louis St-Laurent
- Opera singer Pierette Alarie
- Hockey player Maurice Richard

First performance of O Canada

"O Canada" was performed for the first time on June 24, 1880, in Quebec City. The music was composed by Calixa Lavallée and the first lyrics, in French, were written by Adolphe-Basile Routhier. The tune did not become the country's official national anthem until July 1, 1980.

First Canadian Nobel Prize

You're undoubtedly familiar with author Alice Munro snagging the 2013 Nobel Prize in Literature and becoming the first Canadian to do so. But do you know who was the first Canadian to win any Nobel Prize? That would be Sir Frederick Banting, who discovered insulin (along with his assistant Charles Best and other colleagues), thereby changing the lives of millions of people with diabetes. In 1923—the year after he first injected a patient with insulin—he was awarded the Nobel Prize in Medicine.

Canadian Nobel Prize winners

1.	Ralph Steinman (1943–2011)	Medicine, 2011
2.	Willard S. Boyle (1924–2011)	Physics, 2009
3.	Robert A. Mundell (1932–)	Economics, 1999
4.	Myron S. Scholes (1941–)	Economics, 1996
5.	William Vickrey (1914–96)	Economics, 1996
6.	Bertram N. Brockhouse (1918–2003)	Physics, 1994
7.	Rudolph A. Marcus (1923–)	Chemistry, 1992
8.	Richard E. Taylor (1929–)	Physics, 1990
9.	Sidney Altman (1939–)	Chemistry, 1989
10.	Henry Taube (1915–2005)	Chemistry, 1983
11.	David H. Hubel (1926–)	Medicine, 1981
12.	Saul Bellow* (1915–2005)	Literature, 1976
13.	Charles Brenton Huggins (1901–97)	Medicine, 1966
14.	Lester Bowles Pearson (1897–1972)	Peace, 1957
15.	William Francis Giauque (1895–1982)	Chemistry, 1949
16.	Frederick Grant Banting (1891–1941)	Medicine, 1923
	*Saul Bellow was born in Quebec but later became an American citizen.	

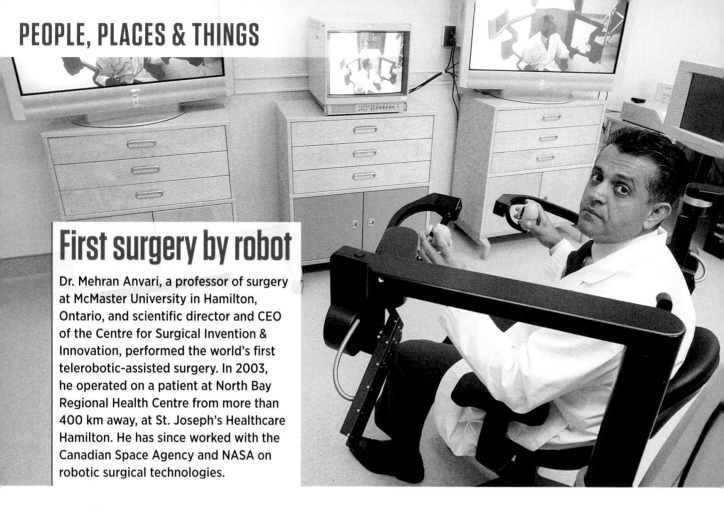

First surgery by robot

Dr. Mehran Anvari, a professor of surgery at McMaster University in Hamilton, Ontario, and scientific director and CEO of the Centre for Surgical Invention & Innovation, performed the world's first telerobotic-assisted surgery. In 2003, he operated on a patient at North Bay Regional Health Centre from more than 400 km away, at St. Joseph's Healthcare Hamilton. He has since worked with the Canadian Space Agency and NASA on robotic surgical technologies.

First vaccination

Dr. John Clinch is believed to have been the first doctor in North America to administer vaccinations. In 1798, the first person he vaccinated was his nephew Joseph Hart. Clinch later vaccinated 700 people for smallpox in Trinity, Newfoundland. Encouraged by the results, doctors in other communities in the province and in Halifax adopted the practice.

First woman doctor

The first Canadian woman to practise medicine in Canada was Emily Stowe of Norwich, Ontario, who started working as a doctor in Toronto in 1867. Her daughter, Augusta Stowe Gullen, was the first woman to earn a medical degree in Canada. She studied at the Toronto School of Medicine and graduated from Victoria College in Cobourg, Ontario, in 1883.

First licensed woman doctor

In 1875, Jennie Trout of Stratford, Ontario, became the first woman in Canada licensed to practise medicine. Trout was encouraged in the endeavour by Emily Stowe (see above). Trout practised at Toronto's Therapeutic and Electrical Institute until 1882.

First birth of pre-sexed calf

The world's first calf born with its sex predetermined in a laboratory came into the world on December 25, 1975, at the Animal Disease Research Institute in Nepean, Ontario. The Holstein heifer (named Eugenia Carol) represented a breakthrough in embryo transfer that was later used with other species.

FIRST DIRECTOR GENERAL OF WORLD HEALTH ORGANIZATION

Canadian Dr. Brock Chisholm, born in Oakville, Ontario, in 1896, was the first director general of the World Health Organization. He served in the position from 1948 to 1953. Chisholm was also the first federal deputy minister of health when the government created the Department of National Health and Welfare in 1944.

First photograph of Canada

What else other than Ontario's Niagara Falls would appear in the first known picture of Canada? It was taken by English industrial chemist H.L. Pattinson during a visit to America. The plate on which the image of Horseshoe Falls appears is marked April 1840 on the back. A total of eight of Pattinson's plates from this trip have been discovered, a number of which show buildings in Niagara Falls, including the Clifton Hotel, which was frequented by dignitaries of the time.

First Women's Institute

The world's first Women's Institute, an organization created to help educate women (especially those living in rural areas) in a wide range of skills, was established in Canada in 1897. After the Stoney Creek Women's Institute was founded in this Ontario community, the concept spread across the nation and the world.

First electric streetlights

Quebec City's Dufferin Terrace was the first area in Canada to have electrical streetlights. The lights debuted in 1883, just three years after the first test of outdoor electrical lighting in North America.

First YMCA

The first YMCA in North America started in Montreal on November 25, 1851. When it began, the Y had strong ties to Protestant churches, but this soon changed as people from all religions were welcomed. The YMCA of Greater Montreal went on to open the first public library in the city in 1854.

Most dinosaurs

Looking for dinosaur bones? The Royal Tyrrell Museum of Palaeontology, near Drumheller, Alberta, has the largest display of dinosaurs on Earth. It's Canada's only museum dedicated to palaeontology. The museum, which opened September 25, 1985, is named after Joseph Burr Tyrrell, who discovered the Albertosaurus in 1884, not far from the museum's site near Kneehill Creek.

Highest restaurant

Talk about dining at the height of style. Eagle's Eye restaurant at the Kicking Horse Mountain Resort near Golden, British Columbia, is the country's highest eatery. Located at the summit of the Golden Eagle Express gondola, it's 2,350 m above sea level. Reservations are highly recommended.

Oldest working birdcage elevator

The Maritime Museum of BC in Victoria features the oldest continuously operating birdcage elevator in North America. The building the museum is housed in was built as the home of the province's first Supreme Court, which opened February 1, 1889. The elevator was installed during a renovation in 1899–1900.

Most Inuit art

Established in 1912, the Winnipeg Art Gallery claims a couple of Canadian superlatives. It's home to the world's largest public collection of contemporary Inuit art, with more than 10,730 works. The gallery also offers the largest program of art classes in the country, with professional artists teaching classes for children and adults.

FIRST LABOUR DAY PARADE

Power to the people. The world's first Labour Day Parade was held on April 15, 1872, in Toronto. The parade was arranged by the Toronto Trades Assembly to protest federal laws against unions and the imprisonment of 24 Toronto Typographical Union members.

First art gallery

Joseph Légaré (see First Canadian landscape painter, below) opened the first art gallery in Canada. The gallery, which featured his personal collection of art, opened in 1833 in Quebec City.

First Canadian landscape painter

Canadian art is well known for its landscape paintings. Artist Joseph Légaré, born in Quebec City in 1795, is considered the first Canadian-born landscape painter. Shown here is his *View of the Fire in Saint-Jean District of Quebec City, Looking West*, painted in 1848.

Largest art school

The Ontario College of Art & Design University, located in Toronto, is the nation's largest art school. Founded in 1876 as the Ontario School of Art, OCAD now hosts some 3,500 full-time students and about 1,000 part-time students, and has an annual budget of $56 million.

Most reference materials

It makes sense that Library and Archives Canada has the world's largest and most important collection of Canadian reference materials. The collection includes:

• more than 71,000 hours of films dating back to 1897
• over 2.5 million architectural drawings
• 3.18 million megabytes of electronic materials
• millions of books
• more than 21.3 million photographs
• over 270,000 hours of video and sound recordings
• more than 343,000 works of art
— and much, much more.

First museum

The first museum in Canada, and the country's oldest, is that of Thomas Barnett, an English "collector" who immigrated to Canada in the early 1820s. He opened a museum of his personal collection of local and foreign artifacts in Niagara Falls in 1827. That museum became today's Niagara Falls Museum.

Biggest museum

The Canadian Museum of History, formerly the Canadian Museum of Civilization, in Gatineau, Quebec, is the nation's largest museum. The museum boasts about 5 million artifacts in its collection, which attracts more than 1.3 million visitors each year.

Most vaudeville scenery

What a scene! Or two or three. The Elgin and Winter Garden Theatre Centre in Toronto is home to the world's largest collection of vaudeville scenery. The backdrops (some of which date back to 1913, when the two theatres opened) were discovered during the facility's restoration, which began in 1987 and was completed in 1989. A number of the pieces are on display at the Centre.

Oldest artists' association

The Royal Canadian Academy of Arts is the country's oldest national professional artists' association. Established in 1880, the organization's aim was the advancement and development of visual arts in Canada.

Biggest gift

The Art Gallery of Ontario's Thomson Collection, some 2,000 works of Canadian and European art collected by Canadian businessman Ken Thomson, is the largest gift ever made to a Canadian cultural institution.

MOST TOTEM POLES

The Canadian Museum of History is home to the world's largest indoor collection of totem poles. Many of the museum's totem poles are housed in the building's dramatic Grand Hall.

MOST CANOES

The Canadian Canoe Museum in Peterborough, Ontario, is home to the world's largest collection of canoes and kayaks. Founded in 1997, the museum has more than 100 watercraft on permanent display, and its total collection of the boats numbers more than 600.

Oldest French university

The Université Laval in Quebec City is the oldest French-language university in North America. Established in 1663, today the school has nearly 50,000 students and more than 270,000 graduates.

Largest living history museum

Want to get a load of history? Try a visit to Fort Edmonton Park, known alternatively as "Canada's largest living history museum" or "the largest historical theme park in Canada." Among the attractions at the 63-hectare park: more than 80 historical buildings, a steam-engine train, four early-1900 streetcars and a stagecoach.

Oldest English university

The oldest public English-language university in Canada — and one of the oldest universities in North America — is the University of New Brunswick. Its Fredericton campus was established in 1785 (the Saint John campus was created in 1964).

FIRST NURSING SCHOOL

Canada's first school for nursing was established in 1874 at Ontario's St. Catharines General Hospital. The program inspired similar training initiatives at hospitals throughout the country.

Biggest university

Talk about student life! The University of Toronto is the country's largest university with enough students to create a small city — more than 82,000 students at three campuses (St. George, Mississauga and Scarborough). U of T offers more than 700 undergraduate programs, 215 graduate programs and 63 professional programs. Its operations budget for 2012–13 was $1.8 billion.

Biggest school board

School's in! And a whole lot of it. The Toronto District School Board is the nation's largest. It educates about 259,000 students (172,000 elementary and 87,000 secondary) at nearly 600 schools throughout the city.

First teaching at patient's bedside

Clinical medical teaching at a patient's bedside was first done in North America at the Montreal General Hospital in 1881.

Oldest university building

The oldest university building in Canada still being used as part of a university campus is Sir Howard Douglas Hall (Old Arts Building) at the University of New Brunswick. The building officially opened on January 1, 1829.

Largest academic library system

The libraries at the University of Toronto constitute the largest academic library system in Canada and the third-largest in North America. U of T has 44 libraries at three campuses that contain more than 12 million publications in 341 languages, 1.5 million electronic resources, 28,000 linear m of archival material and 500 terabytes of data.

Most varieties of spoken English

What did you say? Was that English? Newfoundlanders are known for their distinctive way of speaking. The province is home to more varieties of spoken English than anywhere else on Earth. The province's English dialects are so distinct that there's even a dictionary of Newfoundland English.

First medical school

Montreal General Hospital founded the first medical school in Canada. The Montreal Medical Institute was established in 1825 and became the McGill University Faculty of Medicine in 1829.

Largest library for the blind

The Canadian National Institute for the Blind Library is the largest library of accessible materials for people with print disabilities. The library's collection includes more than 80,000 books in Braille, e-braille, printbraille, e-text, DAISY and online audio; popular audio magazines; research tools such as encyclopedias and dictionaries; and more than 50 regional, national and international newspapers.

RCMP historic training site

All cadets of the Royal Canadian Mounted Police undergo their initial basic training at the RCMP Academy "Depot" Division in Regina. Established in 1885, the site was once the headquarters of the North West Mounted Police and then later, the Royal Northwest Mounted Police.

Largest boys school

Located north of Toronto in Aurora, Ontario, St. Andrew's College is Canada's largest all-boys private school. In 2013, 613 students were enrolled in the school in Grades 5 to 12. The campus is 44 hectares and has 17 buildings. First established in Toronto in 1899, the school moved to its current location in 1926.

Oldest Canadian club outside Canada

The Canada Club in London, England, founded in 1810, is the oldest Canadian club outside of Canada. Originally formed by fur traders of the North West Company, today the club today is open to all with an interest in Canada. It hosts two dinners a year featuring keynote speakers of significance to Canadians. Every Canadian Prime Minister has addressed the club.

First forest research centre

Canada's first forest research centre, Ontario's Petawawa Research Forest, was created in 1918. Still in operation today, it is also the country's oldest continuously operated research forest. In its founding year, the nation's first forest inventory was completed and the first forest sample plots were initiated.

Oldest military school

Today, all cadets at the Royal Military College of Canada in Kingston, Ontario, know the names of the "Old Eighteen," the school's first class of students in 1874. The RMC is the nation's oldest military school, which was founded to train Canadian cadets in all aspects of the military profession.

First social club

L'Ordre de Bon Temps ("Order of Good Cheer") was North America's first social club. It was founded in 1606 in Port-Royal, Nova Scotia, by explorer Samuel de Champlain.

Oldest co-ed boarding school

Albert College in Belleville, Ontario, is Canada's oldest co-educational boarding and day school. Established in 1857, the school educates students from pre-kindergarten to Grade 12 and post graduate. It offers residency to students of both sexes in Grade 7 onward.

Largest science lesson

Canada hosted the world's largest practical science lesson on October 12, 2012, organized by the federal government. The lesson, held at 1 p.m. EST at 88 locations across the country, focused on two experiments demonstrating Bernoulli's Principle on air pressure and included 13,701 students.

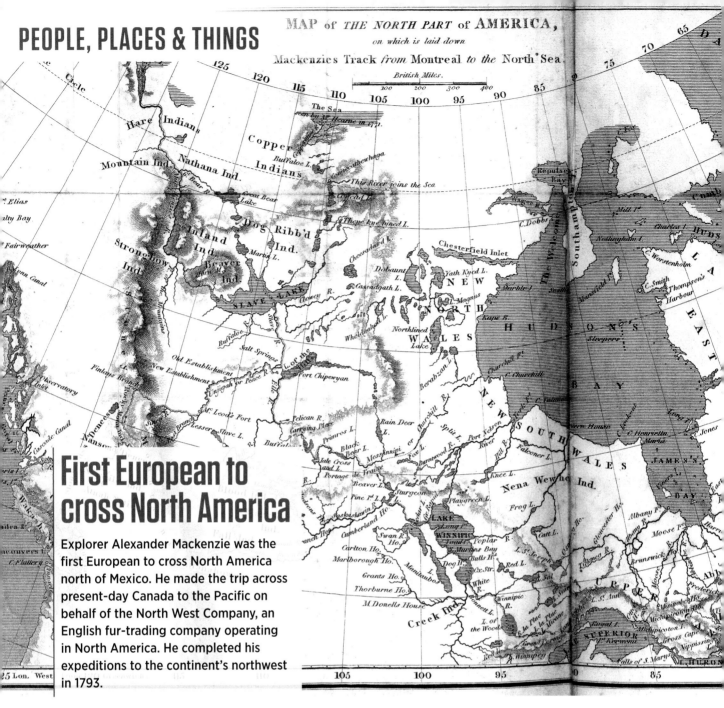

MAP of *THE NORTH PART* of AMERICA,
on which is laid down
Mackenzie's Track *from* Montreal *to* the North Sea.

First European to cross North America

Explorer Alexander Mackenzie was the first European to cross North America north of Mexico. He made the trip across present-day Canada to the Pacific on behalf of the North West Company, an English fur-trading company operating in North America. He completed his expeditions to the continent's northwest in 1793.

Last soldier killed in First World War

It's a terrible distinction. The last soldier killed in battle during the First World War was Canadian Private George Lawrence Prince. Prince died at Mons, Belgium, on November 11, 1918, about two minutes before the signing of the Armistice. He had enlisted in the army just over a year earlier, in October 1917.

First Victoria Cross

Lieutenant Alexander Roberts Dunn was the first Canadian to receive a Victoria Cross, the Commonwealth's highest honour in recognition of military valour. Dunn, born in York (now Toronto), was awarded the medal in 1857 for his role in the Crimean War.

First wheelchair around the world

Man in Motion, no doubt. Canadian Rick Hansen, born on August 26, 1957, in Port Alberni, British Columbia, became world famous in 1985 when he travelled more than 40,000 km around the world through 34 countries in his wheelchair to raise awareness for spinal cord injuries and research. Dubbed the Man in Motion World Tour, Hansen's feat — the first such ever — raised more than $26 million.

Longest-serving prime minister

William Lyon Mackenzie King is Canada's longest-serving prime minister and the longest-serving prime minister in the Commonwealth. He served 21 years over three terms: December 29, 1921 to June 28, 1926; September 25, 1926 to August 7, 1930; and October 23, 1935 to November 15, 1948. King, a Liberal, oversaw the creation of old-age pensions and unemployment insurance and appointed the first woman to the Senate (in 1930), among other accomplishments.

First Aboriginal senator

The first Aboriginal appointed to Canada's Senate was James Gladstone in 1958. Gladstone, a member of the Blood Tribe of the Blackfoot Nation, represented the province of Alberta. When he was appointed, status Indians in the country did not have the right to vote — a right Gladstone helped to fight for, and which was granted in 1960.

First Quints

They brought a whole new meaning to the phrase "Take five." The Dionne quintuplets, born in Corbeil, Ontario, on May 28, 1934, were the first quintuplets in the world to survive more than a few days. They would become the biggest tourist attraction in the nation at the time, generating an estimate $500 million for the province of Ontario and attracting some three million people to see them in person.

First polar dives

You could call him Canada's very own coldwater man. Dr. Joseph MacInnis, born in Barrie, Ontario, on March 2, 1937, led the teams that made the first scientific dives at the North Pole in the 1970s.

Northernmost shipwreck

Dr. Joseph MacInnis wasn't done yet! In 1980, MacInnis led the team that discovered the world's northernmost shipwreck. On August 13, the remains of the *Breadalbane* — a Royal Navy ship that sank in August 1853 while delivering supplies to another expedition — were found by MacInnis' crew near Nunavut's Beechy Island.

First polar undersea station

Dr. Joseph MacInnis also built the world's first polar undersea station. Dubbed the *Sub-Igloo*, the capsule had room for four and was established under the ice in the Northwest Passage in 1972.

Deepest dive

Now here's a story with depth. James Cameron, born in Kapuskasing, Ontario, and the director of the Oscar-winning films *Titanic* and *Avatar*, became the first person to dive solo to the deepest part of the world's oceans. On March, 26, 2012, Cameron visited the Mariana Trench in the Pacific Ocean, some 11 km below the surface, in a custom-built submarine, *Deepsea Challenger*.

Youngest skier to the South Pole

In 2004, when she was 18, Iqaluit native Sarah McNair-Laundry became the youngest person in the world to ski to the South Pole. The more than 1,100 km trek took her 52 days to complete.

First Canadian spaceman

Quebec City native Marc Garneau became the first Canadian to fly in space on October 5, 1984. Garneau was a payload specialist on NASA shuttle mission 41-G. He returned to space in 1996 and 2000, and in total logged more than 677 hours in space.

First Canadian space commander

Astronaut Chris Hadfield became the first Canadian to command a spaceship on March 13, 2013. Hadfield was Commander of the International Space Station during the second part of his five-month stay there. Hadfield's mission ended on May 13, 2013, after 146 days in space (144 on the ISS). He travelled nearly 99.8 million km during his mission.

First Canadian spacewoman

On January 22, 1992, Dr. Roberta Bondar, a native of Sault Ste. Marie, Ontario, became the first Canadian woman in space and the second Canadian to leave the planet. During her eight-day mission on the space shuttle *Discovery*, Bondar conducted experiments to help find ways to allow future astronauts to take prolonged flights.

Youngest supernova-spotter

How do you top finding a supernova—the most luminous type of cataclysmic explosion of a dying star—as a 10-year-old? You keep looking for more. That's exactly what Nathan Gray of Greenwood, Nova Scotia, vowed to do after spotting potential supernova PGC 61330 in the constellation of Draco on October 30, 2013. If the International Astronomical Union confirms Gray's discovery, he'll become the youngest known person to locate a supernova—besting the previous record holder, his sister Kathryn, by just 33 days.

FIRST BLACK HOLE

Dr. Tom Bolton was the first to discover a black hole. Bolton discovered Cygnus X-1 from the David Dunlap Observatory, just north of Toronto, in 1971.

Canadian birth rate

Here's how all Canada's provinces rank on birth rate, based on 2011 data from Statistics Canada:

	Fertility rate*
Canada	1.61
Nunavut	2.97
Saskatchewan	1.99
Northwest Territories	1.97
Manitoba	1.86
Alberta	1.81
Yukon	1.73
Quebec	1.69
Prince Edward Island	1.62
Ontario	1.52
New Brunswick	1.54
Nova Scotia	1.47
Newfoundland and Labrador	1.45
British Columbia	1.42
*Average number of children per woman	

Highest birth rate

Based on 2011 data from Statistics Canada, Nunavut has Canada's highest birth rate, at an average of 2.97 children per woman.

Lowest birth rate

British Columbia has the country's lowest birth rate, at an average of 1.42 children per woman, according to 2011 data from Statistics Canada.

Most births

Perhaps not surprisingly, given that it's home to the largest provincial population, Ontario leads the country in total births, with 140,135 (based on 2011 data from Statistics Canada).

Fewest births

The Yukon Territory has the lowest number of births, based on 2011 data from Statistics Canada, at just 431.

Largest youth-driven charity

Free the Children, founded by brothers Craig and Marc Kielburger in 1995 in Thornhill, Ontario, is the world's largest youth-driven charity.

Highest median age

Newfoundland and Labrador has the nation's highest median age, at 43.8 years, based on Statistics Canada data from 2011. The median age is the exact age where half the population is older and half is younger.

Youngest territory

Nunavut has Canada's lowest median age, 24.8 years, based on 2011 data from Statistics Canada. Nearly one-third (31.5 percent) of the territory's residents are under the age of 15.

Highest after-tax income

Want to keep more of your money? Move to Alberta. That province has the nation's highest median after-tax income.

Canadian life expectancy

The life expectancy of the average Canadian at birth is 81.1 years, according to the United Nation's Human Development Reports.

Biggest energy users

According to a 2013 report from The Conference Board of Canada (*How Canada Performs—Environment*), Canadians are the largest users of energy in the developed world.

Last executions

The last executions in Canada made under the Criminal Code occurred on December 11, 1962. Ronald Turpin, 29, and Arthur Lucas, 54, were hanged at the Don Jail in Toronto. Turpin had been convicted of murdering a Toronto police officer, while Lucas had been convicted of murdering an FBI informant.

LAST WOMAN EXECUTED

The last woman executed in Canada under the Criminal Code, Marguerite Pitre, was hanged in 1953. Pitre had been convicted as a co-conspirator in Canada's largest mass murder at the time.

Most garbage

Here's a dirty secret. Canada produces more municipal waste than any other developed nation, according to a 2013 report from The Conference Board of Canada (see above). Each Canadian produced 777 kg of municipal garbage in 2008, and the amount of waste generated by the country per capita has steadily increased since 1990.

Last fatal duel

Draw! The last fatal duel in Canada occurred on May 22, 1838, in Verdun, Quebec, then part of Lower Canada. Major Henry Warde was fatally shot by lawyer Robert Sweeny. Warde's offence? A love letter to Mrs. Sweeny.

Most salt

That's salty. Canada has the world's largest per capita use of salt. It's estimated that each Canadian uses more than 360 kg of salt annually. Salt as a de-icing agent makes up a large part of this figure.

Citize
Immig.

enneté et
tion Canada

The most immigrants

Ontario is home to the largest proportion of people born outside Canada, according to the latest data from Statistics Canada. About 3.6 million immigrants reside in Ontario, 53 percent of the nation's total.

Fees
Mailir
What

Most Icelanders

Given its reputation as being particularly cold (temperature-wise), is it any wonder that Manitoba is home to the largest Icelandic population outside of Iceland? Between 1870 and 1915, 20,000 Icelanders immigrated to the province—nearly a quarter of Iceland's population at the time. Today Manitoba's provincial government continues to appeal to Icelanders to settle there.

Most Asians

Canada is a nation largely built on immigration. Based on the latest data from Statistics Canada, the largest source of immigrants in recent years is from Asia (including the Middle East). About 57 percent of all immigrants who arrived between 2006 and 2011 came from Asia, a total of nearly 660,000 people.

Most South Asians

Canada is home to people from all over the world. Based on the latest data from Statistics Canada, nearly 20 percent of the country's population identifies as a visible minority. The largest group is South Asian. There are a total of 1,567,400 individuals who identify as such, which makes up one-quarter of all visible minorities in the country and nearly five percent of the nation's total population.

More Chinese speakers

Chinese languages are the most common among immigrants to Canada whose first language is other than French or English, according to the latest data from Statistics Canada. About 850,000 individuals reported a Chinese language as their mother tongue, 13 percent of all foreign-born residents for whom French or English isn't a first language.

More Christians

More than 22 million people, roughly two-thirds of Canada's population, report affiliations with a Christian religion, based on the latest data from Statistics Canada. The largest Christian group is Roman Catholics, at 12.7 million people.

First Christmas tree

O, Canada, O Christmas Tree. The first Christmas tree in Canada was set up on Christmas Eve, 1781, in Sorel, Quebec, north of Montreal. The balsam fir was decorated with fruit and lit with white candles.

Canadians' favourite American state

Canadians aren't shy about visiting our neighbours to the south. But do you know which American state is most visited by Canadians, according to Statistics Canada? New York State saw 3.4 million overnight visits from Canadians in 2010. Florida was second with 3.1 million overnight visits, while Washington State was third with 2.3 million.

Canadians' second-favourite destination

Do you know the most popular foreign destination for Canadians after the United States? Mexico. Canadians made nearly 1.4 million overnight visits there in 2010, according to Statistics Canada.

Most visited nation

The most-visited overseas nation by Canadians? United Kingdom, where Canadians made 880,000 overnight visits in 2010, according to Statistics Canada.

Most expensive state

Hmm, what could possibly be responsible for this? Based on Statistics Canada data from 2010, Canadians spent more money (an average $188 per night) in Nevada — home of Lost Wages, er, Las Vegas — than in any other American state.

Most compelling state

Canadians travelling to the United States stay longest in Florida (an average of 17.4 overnights per visit), according to 2010 data from Statistics Canada.

Worst epidemic

Canada's worst epidemic? Spanish influenza, brought home in 1918 by soldiers returning from the First World War. The Spanish flu killed some 50,000 Canadians. Worldwide, it's believed to have claimed the lives of more people than the Great War itself.

Worst rockslide

The worst rockslide in Canadian history occurred on April 29, 1903, when 82 million tonnes of rock crashed down from the Turtle Mountain on the town of Frank, Alberta. The slide killed 70 people.

WORST FOREST FIRES

During what's considered the hottest recorded year in Canada (1988), the forest fires were the costliest in the country's history. An estimated 10,560 fires destroyed 4.6 million hectares of forests, approximately 50 percent more than an average year.

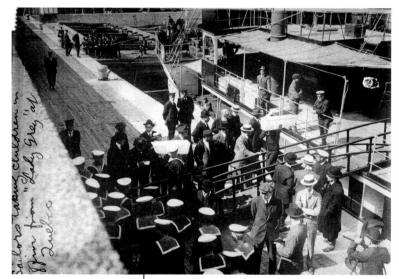

Worst shipwreck

The worst maritime disaster in Canadian history was the sinking of the *Empress of Ireland* in the St. Lawrence River near Rimouski, Quebec, on May 29, 1914. A total of 1,014 people died when the ship collided with the Norwegian collier *Storstad* in the fog.

Worst explosion

The world's largest accidental explosion (and Canada's worst disaster) was the Halifax Explosion of December 6, 1917. Some 1,600 people were killed, another 9,000 injured and 6,000 left homeless in the disaster, caused when the French munitions carrier, *Mont Blanc*, and the Belgian relief vessel, *Imo*, collided in the harbour's Narrows.

Biggest planned explosion

Ripple Rock was a killer. More than 20 large ships and at least 100 smaller vessels were sunk or damaged by the underwater mountain in the Seymour Narrows near Campbell River, British Columbia, and 114 people lost their lives as a result. So on April 5, 1958, Ripple Rock became the site of the world's largest peacetime non-atomic explosion, when it was blown up to prevent further accidents.

First recorded avalanche

The first recorded avalanche in Canada and possibly North America, occurred near Nain, Labrador, in 1782. It's believed 22 people died in the snow slide, an account of which was discovered by historian Wallace J. McLean. A postscript in a letter from the Moravian Mission reported the event as "a monstrous body of snow which shot all at once down and pressed the winter hauss even with the ground, with all the people in it excepting one man who was buried in the snow without. Out of 31 only 9 got out alive."

Deadliest avalanche

The deadliest avalanche in Canadian history occurred on March 5, 1910, when 62 railway workers were killed two km west of Rogers Pass, British Columbia. Their engine was hit by a snow slide and hurtled 500 m into Bear Creek. More than 600 volunteers dug through 10 m of snow with shovels and pickaxes in search of survivors.

Worst encounter with an iceberg

The world's worst iceberg accident? The reportedly "unsinkable" *Titanic* hit an iceberg on April 14, 1912, 700 km southeast of Newfoundland, and 1,500 people died in the waters of the north Atlantic. The disaster is considered one of the planet's worst maritime disasters ever.

Worst flood

The Red River Flood in the spring of 1950 is considered the greatest flood disaster in Canadian history. The river crested 9.2 m above its normal level in Winnipeg. Just one person drowned, but the flood forced the evacuation of 100,000 people from southern Manitoba, damaged 5,000 homes and buildings, and cost $550 million in property damage. Following the disaster, the provincial government decided to build the Winnipeg Floodway to mitigate future flooding.

Deadliest train wreck

Canada's deadliest train disaster occurred on June 29, 1864, near St-Hilaire, Quebec, on the Grand Truck Railway. It's believed 99 passengers were killed and another 100 injured when the train — carrying 458 people, largely German and Polish immigrants — plunged into the Richelieu River after failing to stop for an open swing bridge.

Deadliest earthquake

The deadliest recorded earthquake in Canadian history claimed 27 lives, all of whom drowned in the resulting tsunami that hit Newfoundland's Burin Pennisula. Centered near the Laurentian slope, offshore between Newfoundland and Nova Scotia, the 7.2 magnitude quake struck on November 18, 1929.

Worst offshore earthquake

The largest recorded earthquake in the country was an 8.1 magnitude quake that struck offshore near British Columbia's Haida Gwaii islands on August 22, 1949. Considered one of the largest quakes ever, the tremor fortunately did not cause any deaths, although the shaking was so significant it was said to have knocked cows off their feet on Haida Gwaii.

Worst onshore earthquake

The largest recorded onshore earthquake in Canadian history occurred on June 23, 1946, on Vancouver Island. The epicentre of the 7.3 magnitude quake was in the Forbidden Plateau area in central Vancouver Island. It caused considerable damage in many island communities, including Comox, Port Alberni and Powell River, and resulted in one death (a drowning caused by a wave that capsized a small boat).

Longest beard

Sarwan Singh of Surrey, British Columbia, has the longest beard in the world according to Guinness World Records. Singh's beard, measured on March 4, 2010, was 2.37 m long.

Aircraft pulling

Kevin Fast of Cobourg, Ontario, holds the distinction of the heaviest aircraft pull in the world, according to Guinness World Records. Fast pulled a CC-173 Globemaster III, weighing 188.83 tonnes, 8.8 m at Canadian Forces Base Trenton, in Trenton, Ontario, on September 17, 2009.

Balancing spoons on face

Aaron Caissie of Winnipeg can balance more spoons on his face than anyone in the world, according to Guinness World Records. Caissie set the mark of 17 on April 18, 2009.

MOST SOCCER BALL TOUCHES – 60 SECONDS

According to Guinness World Records, Canadian Chloe Hegland holds the record for most touches of a soccer ball (while keeping it in the air) in one minute by a female—339. She set the record on November 3, 2007, while filming a Guinness special in Beijing, China.

MOST SOCCER BALL TOUCHES – 30 SECONDS

Hegland (see above) also holds the record for most touches of a soccer ball (while keeping it in the air) in 30 seconds by a female (163), according to Guinness World Records. Hegland achieved the feat on February 23, 2008.

Heavy over 100

Kevin Fast (see Aircraft pulling) also holds the record for the heaviest vehicle pulled over 100 feet, according to Guinness World Records. On September 15, 2008, Fast pulled a 57,243kg vehicle more than 30.48 m over level ground.

Chainsaw juggling

Aaron Gregg of Victoria achieved the most chainsaw juggling catches ever (88), according to Guinness World Records. Gregg set the record on July 28, 2008.

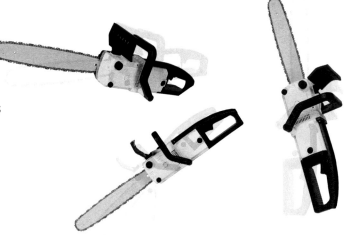

WORLD'S LARGEST AXE
Nackawic, New Brunswick

WORLD'S LARGEST BEAVER
Beaverlodge, Alberta

WORLD'S LARGEST BADMINTON RACKET
St. Albert, Alberta

WORLD'S LARGEST BEE
Falher, Alberta

WORLD'S LARGEST BLUEBERRY
Oxford, Nova Scotia

WORLD'S LARGEST BUNNOCK
Macklin, Saskatchewan

WORLD'S LARGEST BURL
Port McNeil, British Columbia

WORLD'S LARGEST CHAINSAW
Lillooet, British Columbia

WORLD'S LARGEST ADIRONDACK CHAIR
Varney, Ontario

WORLD'S LARGEST MUSKOKA CHAIR
Gravenhurst, Ontario

WORLD'S LARGEST CHUCK WAGON
Dewberry, Alberta

WORLD'S LARGEST CLAIM POST
Cobalt, Ontario

WORLD'S LARGEST COOKIE JAR
Deloraine, Manitoba

WORLD'S LARGEST CROSS-COUNTRY SKIS
100 Mile House, British Columbia

WORLD'S LARGEST CURLING ROCK
Arborg, Manitoba

WORLD'S LARGEST COKE CAN
Portage La Prairie, Manitoba

WORLD'S LARGEST CONCH
Caraquet, New Brunswick

WORLD'S LARGEST CUCKOO CLOCK
Kimberley, British Columbia

WORLD'S LARGEST DINOSAUR
Drumheller, Alberta

WORLD'S LARGEST DRAGONFLY
Wabamun, Alberta

WORLD'S LARGEST ENDANGERED FERRUGIOUS HAWK
Leader, Saskatchewan

WORLD'S LARGEST ILLUMINATED FIDDLE
Sydney, Nova Scotia

WORLD'S LARGEST FIDDLEHEADS
Plaster Rock, New Brunswick

WORLD'S LARGEST FIRE HYDRANT
Elm Creek, Manitoba

WORLD'S LARGEST FLY ROD
Houston, British Columbia

WORLD'S LARGEST GOLD PAN
Quesnel, British Columbia

WORLD'S LARGEST GOLF BAG
Orangeville, Ontario

WORLD'S LARGEST GOLF TEE
Trochu, Alberta

CANADA'S LARGEST GOOSE
Wawa, Ontario

WORLD'S LARGEST HOCKEY STICK AND PUCK
Duncan, Alberta

WORLD'S LARGEST HONEYBEE
Tisdale, Saskatchewan

WORLD'S LARGEST INUKSHUK
Schomberg, Ontario.

WORLD'S LARGEST LAMP
Donalda, Alberta.

WORLD'S LARGEST LOBSTER
Shediac, New Brunswick

WORLD'S LARGEST MALLARD
Andrew, Alberta

WORLD'S LARGEST MAPLE LEAF
Millville, New Brunswick

WORLD'S LARGEST MOOSE
Moose Jaw, Saskatchewan

WORLD'S LARGEST WOODEN NICKEL
Boiestown, New Brunswick

WORLD'S LARGEST OIL CAN
Rocanville, Saskatchewan

WORLD'S LARGEST ORCHARD LADDER
Summerland, British Columbia

WORLD'S LARGEST PAINTING ON EASEL
Altona, Manitoba

FXS-1996-A

WORLD'S LARGEST PAPER CLIP
Kipling, Saskatchewan

WORLD'S LARGEST PEROGY
Glendon, Alberta

WORLD'S SECOND LARGEST SMOKING PIPE
Saint Claude, Manitoba

WORLD'S LARGEST PURPLE MARTIN COLONY
Neepawa, Manitoba

WORLD'S LARGEST PUTTER
Bow Island, Alberta

THE WALL (WORLD'S LARGEST PHOTO-MOSAIC)
Port Carling, Ontario

WORLD'S LARGEST RAILROAD SPIKE
Hines Creek, Alberta

WORLD'S LARGEST ROOSTER
Shediac, New Brunswick

WORLD'S LARGEST SILVER FOX
Salisbury, New Brunswick

WORLD'S LARGEST SNOWMAN
Beardmore, Ontario

WORLD'S LARGEST SOFTBALL
Chauvin, Alberta

WORLD'S LARGEST STARSHIP ENTERPRISE
Vulcan, Alberta

WORLD'S LARGEST STURGEON
Dominion City, Manitoba

WORLD'S LARGEST SUNDIAL
Lloydminster, Saskatchewan

WORLD'S TALLEST TEEPEE
Medicine Hat, Alberta

WORLD'S LARGEST TIN SOLDIER
New Westminster, British Columbia

WORLD'S LARGEST TOMAHAWK
Cut Knife, Saskatchewan

WORLD'S LARGEST TOTEM POLE
Alert Bay, British Columbia

WORLD'S LARGEST TOTEM POLE FROM A SINGLE TREE
Victoria, British Columbia

WORLD'S LARGEST TOTEM POLE IN DIAMETER
Duncan, British Columbia

WORLD'S LARGEST TREE CRUSHER
Mackenzie, British Columbia

CANADA'S LARGEST TURTLE
Turtleford, Saskatchewan

WORLD'S LARGEST UKRAINIAN EASTER EGG
Vegreville, Alberta

WORLD'S LARGEST WAGON WHEEL AND PICK
Fort Assiniboine, Alberta

WORLD'S LARGEST TRACTOR WEATHER VANE
Westlock, Alberta

WORLD'S LARGEST WESTERN BOOT
Edmonton, Alberta

PHOTO CREDITS

b = bottom; t = top; l = left; r= right; m= middle;
bi= background image; ip: inset photo

Associated Press

pp. 104-105: ©ASSOCIATED PRESS; p. 153: ©ASSOCIATED PRESS; pp. 112 ml: ©AP Photo/Hibernia Management Co.; pp. 116-117 bi: ©ASSOCIATED PRESS/Jeffrey Ulbrich; p. 133: © ASSOCIATED PRESS/PR NEWSWIRE; pp. 156-157 bi: ©Bettman/Corbis/AP Images; pp. 168-169 bi: ©ASSOCIATED PRESS/Canadian Press/Darryl Dyck; pp. 172-173 bi: ©ASSOCIATED PRESS/Staff/Len Putnam; p. 176: ©ASSOCIATED PRESS/NBC-TV; p. 177: ©Bettmann/Corbis/AP Images; pp. 178-179: ©ASSOCIATED PRESS; p. 181 tr: ©ASSOCIATED PRESS/Rex Features; p. 181 br: ©ASSOCIATED PRESS; p. 183 br: ©ASSOCIATED PRESS/Marty Reichenthal; pp. 196-197 bi: ©ASSOCIATED PRESS/Mary Altaffer; p. 196: ©Bettmann/CORBIS/AP Images; pp. 200-201 bi: ©ASSOCIATED PRESS/Frank Gunn; pp. 200: ©ASSOCIATED PRESS; p. 202: ©ASSOCIATED PRESS/Bebeto Matthews; pp. 204-205 bi: ©ASSOCIATED PRESS/Rick Eglinton/CP; pp. 208-209 bi: ©ASSOCIATED PRESS; p. 215 br: ©ASSOCIATED PRESS/Koji Sasahara; pp. 216-217: ©Bettmann/Corbis/AP Images; p. 233 t: ©ASSOCIATED PRESS/Mikhail Metzel

Can Stock Photo

pp. 20-21: ©Can Stock Photo Inc./Eppic

Corbis

p. 178: ©John Springer Collection/CORBIS; p. 179: ©John Springer Collection/CORBIS; pp. 181-183 bi: ©Neil Preston/CORBIS; pp. 190-191 bi: ©Paul A. Souders/CORBIS; pp. 192-193 bi: ©Bettmann/CORBIS/John Gralak; pp. 194-195 bi: ©Bettmann/CORBIS; p. 194: ©Bettmann/CORBIS; pp. 210-211 bi: ©Gilbert Lundt; Jean-Yves Ruszniewski/TempSport/Corbis; pp. 212-213 bi: ©ANDY CLARK/Reuters/Corbis; p. 232 b: ©Stephen Kraly/Splash News/Corbis

Dreamstime

p. 63: Dreamstime©Jason A. Paul; pp. 188-189 bi: Dreamstime©Marcus Miranda; p. 189: Dreamstime©Matthew Bamberg

iStock

p. 127: istock©duncan1890; p. 137: istock©powerofforever; p. 143: istock©pongky.n; p. 144: istock©alicat; p. 148: istock©Lokibaho; p. 161: istock©DavidBukach

Miscellaneous

p. 87: Courtesy of Michael Mouland; pp. 140-141 bi: © J. Armand Bombardier Museum; pp. 142-143 bi: Courtesy of Library and Archives Canada; pp. 146-147: Courtesy of NASA; pp. 160-161 bi: Public Domain courtesy of the City of Vancouver Archives; p. 160: Public Domain courtesy of the United States Library of Congress's Prints and Photographs Division; p. 164: Courtesy of The Colby Curtis Museum & The Stanstead Historical Society; pp. 180-181 bi: Courtesy of Scholastic Canada; back cover t: Courtesy of NASA

Reuters

p. 147: ©REUTERS/J.P. Moczuiski; p. 184: ©REUTERS; p. 198: ©REUTERS/Andrew Wallace; p. 207: ©REUTERS/Jim Young; p. 209: ©REUTERS/Patrick Price

THE CANADIAN PRESS

pp. 62-63 bi: THE CANADIAN PRESS/Tim Clark; pp. 64-65 bi: THE CANADIAN PRESS/Jacques Boissinot; pp. 92-93 bi: THE CANADIAN PRESS/The Globe and Mail/Deborah Baic; pp. 130-131 ip: THE CANADIAN PRESS/Peter Bregg; p. 191: THE CANADIAN PRESS/Emma Albani; p. 197: THE CANADIAN PRESS/Frank Gunn; p. 220: THE CANADIAN PRESS/The Globe and Mail/Tibor Kolley; p. 232 t: THE CANADIAN PRESS/Robert Flemming; p. 241: THE CANADIAN PRESS

Wikipedia

p. 15 br: Ansgar Walk CC By-SA 2.5/Wikipedia; pp. 106-107 bg: Pierre Bona CC BY-SA 3.0/Wikipedia; p. 118 bl: Lisest CC BY-SA 3.0; p. 121: Public Domain/Wikipedia; p. 125: Public Domain/Windsor then Windsor Now; p. 126: Public Domain; p. 129: Public Domain; p. 130: Public Domain; pp. 148-149 bi: William Hook CC BY-SA 2.0/Wikipedia; p. 149: David Carroll CC BY 2.0/Wikipedia; p. 152: CC BY-SA 3.0/Wikipedia; p. 167: Danielle Scott CC BY 2.0/Wikimedia; p. 170: Public Domain/Wikipedia; p. 171 tr: Public Domain/Wikimedia; br: Public Domain/Wikimedia; p. 174: Bryan C. Passifiume CC BY-SA 3.0/Wikimedia; p. 207 t: D'Arcy Norman CC BY 2.0/Wikipedia; p. 217: ideogibs CC BY-SA 2.0/Wikipedia; p. 219: Public Domain/Wikipedia; p. 221 tr: Public Domain/Wikipedia; br: Denis Jacquerye CC BY-SA 2.0/Wikipedia; p. 224: Public Domain/Wikimedia; p. 225 tr: Wojciech Dittwald CC BY-SA 3.0; br: P199 CC BY-SA 3.0/Wikimedia; p. 230 tl: CC BY 2.0/Wikimedia; p. 231 tl: Jeff Seifred CC BY-SA 2.0/Wikimedia; tr: Public Domain/Wikipedia; p. 233 m: Public Domain/Wikimedia; p. 239 t: Public Domain; br: Public Domain/Wikimedia; p. 240: Public Domain/Wikimedia; p. 242: Public Domain/Wikimedia; p. 243: Dennis Jarvis CC BY-SA 2.0/Wikimedia; p. 244: Antony Stanley CC BY-SA 2.0/Wikimedia; p. 245: Mark Seymour CC BY 2.0/Wikimedia; pp. 246-247 bi: Canoe1967 CC BY 3.0/Wikimedia; p. 248: Public Domain/Wikipedia; p. 249: Public Domain/Wikipedia; back cover br: Public Domain/Wikipedia

Shutterstock

p. 5: © BGSmith; p. 6: © Josef Hanus; p. 8: © Elena Elisseeva; p. 11: © BGSmith; pp. 12-13: © M.M.G.; p. 13: © Albert Pego; pp. 14-15: © Ray Yang; pp. 16-17: © Colin D. Young; pp. 18-19: © puttsk; p. 19: © Elena Elisseeva; p. 21: © 2009fotofriends; pp. 22-23: © Josef Hanus; p. 22: © rook76; pp. 24-25: © ostill; pp. 26-27: © John Brueske; p. 27 t: © Boris15; p. 27 b: © Rainer Lesniewski; p. 29: © Andrew Park; pp. 28-29: © Artifan; pp. 30-31: © Tyler Olson; p. 31: © Rainier Lesniewski; p. 32: © SF photo; p. 33: © Pi-Lens; pp. 32-33: © marevos imaging; p. 34: © Kevin_Hsieh; pp. 34-35: © alan dyer; pp. 36-37: © Protasov AN; p. 37: © Horst Petzoid; pp. 38-39: © Meg Wallace Photography; p. 39: © Jeff Whyte; pp. 40-41: © Chris Hill; p. 43: © Jeff Whyte; pp. 42-43: © David P. Lewis; pp. 44-45: © SurangaSL; pp. 46-47: © Ryan Morgan; p. 47: © JamesChen; p. 49: © Atomazul; p. 48-49: © Blaze986; pp. 50-51: © MountainHardcore; pp. 52-53: © Paul Vasarhelyi; pp. 54-55: © Maridav; pp. 56-57: © 2009fotofriends; pp. 58-59: © Elena Elisseeva; pp. 60-61: © MountainHardcore; pp. 66-67: © AndreAnita; p. 67 t: © Pi-Lens; p. 67 b: © Dennis Donohue; p. 68: © Wolfgang Kruck; pp. 68-69: © Chris Frost; pp. 70-71: © Chiyacat; pp. 72-73: © Sergey Uryadnikov; p. 73 t: © Randimal; p. 73 b: © Cindy Creighton; p. 74 m: © Pete Spiro; p. 74 top: © Ian Maton; p. 75: Piotr Krzeslak; pp. 74-75: © Critterbiz; pp. 76-77: ©claffra; p. 76: © Alexandr Vlassyuk; p. 77: © Lightspring; pp. 78-79: © ValeStock; pp. 80-81: © kzww; p. 81: © aleksandr hunta; pp. 82-83: © Canadapanda; pp. 84-85: © Mars Evis; pp. 86-87: © dreamcatcher; pp. 88-89: © meunierd; p. 89: ©: meunierd; pp. 90-91: © nienora; p. 91: © Georgios Kollidas; p. 93: © Blaze986; pp. 94-95: © 2009fotofriends; p. 95: © Paul McKinnon; pp. 96-97: © Ritu Manoj Jethani; p. 96: © Peter Albrektsen; pp. 98-99: © Andre Nantel; p. 99: © GVictoria; pp. 100-101: © Nagel Photography; p. 101: © e X p o s e; pp. 102-103: © Pictureguy; p. 103: © Lester Balajadia; p. 104: © Max Lindenthaler; p. 105: © Paul MaKinnon; pp. 104-105: © LunaseeStudios; p. 106: © siraphat; p. 107: © bikeriderlondon;

p. 108 t: © Lester Balajadia; p. 108 m: © Kletr; pp. 110-111: © SARIN KUNTHONG; p. 111: © Pi-Lens; pp. 112-113: © SF photo; p. 113: © Ekaterina Garyuk; p. 115: © Eric Isselee; pp. 114-115: © Johanna Goodyear; p. 114: © Paul Binet; p. 117: © V.J. Matthew; pp. 118-119: © Randi Scott; p. 118 top: © SpaceKris; p. 121 middle left: © matka_Wariatka; pp. 120-121: © Constantine Androsoff; pp. 122-123: © Paul McKinnon; pp. 124-125: © I. Pilon; p. 124: © ValeStock; pp. 126-127: © Norman Pogson; pp. 128-129: © Everett Collection; pp. 130-131: © vita khorzhevska; pp. 132-133: © rook76; p. 135: © stocksolutions; pp. 134-135: © Marbury; pp. 136-137: © Jeff Wasserman; p. 137: © Marie C Fields; p. 138 top: © Bombaert Patrick; p. 138 bottom: © Carolina K. Smith MD; p. 139: © Olivier Le Queinec; pp. 138-139: © Michael C. Gray; pp. 144-145: © javarman; p. 145: © Simon Laprida; p. 151: © keki; pp. 150-151: © khuruzero; pp. 152-153: © Roberto Caucino; pp. 154-155: © Nancy Bauer; p. 155: © Sanne vd Berg Fotografie; pp. 158-159: © Josef Hanus; pp. 162-163: © Songquan Deng; p. 163: © Benoit Daoust; p. 165: © Christian Delbert; pp. 164-165: © Scott Prokop; pp. 166-167: © oksana.perkins; p. 167 top: © Modfos; p. 169 bottom right: © Lana B; pp. 170-171: © LaiQuocAnh; p. 173: © David Acosta Allely; pp. 174-175: © Serjio74; pp. 176-177: © holbox; p. 185: © s_bukley; pp. 184-185: © meunierd; pp. 186-187: © igor kisselev; p. 187: © Maridav; p. 186: © Canadapanda; p. 198: © ropsy; p. 199: © Lorraine Swanson; pp. 198-199: © Haslam Photography; pp. 202-203: © Everett Collection; p. 203: © Debby Wong; p. 213: © Roger Asbury; pp. 214-215: © Matthew Jacques; pp. 218-219: © wjarek; pp. 222-223: © Ronnie Chua; p. 226: © Bruce Raynor; pp. 226-227: © Pete Spiro; pp. 228-229: © Zoran Karapancev; pp. 234-235: © Tatyana Vyc; p. 236 bi: © rhfletcher; p. 236 top inset: © Marjan Apostolovic; p. 236 bottom inset: © Elena Elisseeva; p. 237: © alexskopie; p. 238: © Patrick Poendi; p. 242 bottom: © Yanas; front cover: © Furtseff; back cover bl: © AndreAnita; back cover bm: © khuruzero; back cover mt: © igor kisselev; back cover mb: © Josef Hanus

INDEX